Chords & Progressions
Jazz & Popular Guitar

By Arnie Berle.

Cover Design and Art Direction by Mike Bell (UK).
Photography by Peter Wood (UK).
Book design and layout by Mirror Mountain Productions (USA).
Edited by Ronnie Ball (USA).

Order No. AM 61565
US International Standard Book Number: 0.8256.1056.7
UK International Standard Book Number: 0.7119.1076.6

Music Sales America

DISTRIBUTED BY

HAL•LEONARD®
CORPORATION

7777 W. BLUEMOUND RD. P.O.BOX 13819 MILWAUKEE, WI 53213

Table of Contents

4

Introduction

Up until the explosion of rock music in the Fifties, guitar playing was left to the "greats" . . . Lonnie Johnson, Django Reinhardt, Barney Kessel, Herb Ellis to name but a few. It took the success of stars such as Elvis Presley, Bill Haley, and Buddy Holly during the "Rock 'n' Roll era" to make young people all over the world realise that the guitar was an exciting instrument, accessible to all.

By the Sixties, with established "guitar groups" such as The Beatles, The Rolling Stones and The Beach Boys at the forefront of the music scene, the guitar had become the most popular instrument worldwide.

Each style of guitar playing incorporates its own repertoire of chords . . . open string chords, barre chords, extended notes and so forth. As more and more styles were developed, they gradually began to "cross over," creating a whole host of new and exciting sounds. Rock players started experimenting with the more sophisticated jazz guitar chords, while jazz players began to include more open string chords in their repertoires.

Nowadays the guitarist is even more keen to expand his knowledge of different chord styles, as today's new sounds call for skill in all the styles of guitar playing which had been invented several decades ago.

People learning the guitar often face the confusing problem of having a limitless number of chords to master. Chords should be dealt with in relation to each other, not as sets of isolated chord formations and fingerings. The purpose of this book is to teach chord forms for each style of guitar playing in the most practical way possible, whilst broadening the player's knowledge and range of guitar chord skills at the same time.

Right Hand Technique

Although there are many kinds of chords that can be played on the guitar, the ways in which the chords are played are more limited. Below is a brief discussion of some of the techniques which may be used to play the chords shown in this book.

Using the Thumb

The simplest way to play a chord on the guitar is just to strike the strings downward with the thumb. Playing with the thumb produces a soft sound because of the soft impact of the fleshy thumb coming in contact with the strings. While this is not favored by most jazz players, one of the greatest of all jazz guitarists, Wes Montgomery, used just his thumb.

Using the Pick

The most commonly accepted way of playing the guitar is with a pick. The pick is held between the thumb and the index finger. Picks are made of various materials and come in a variety of thicknesses and sizes. It takes some experimenting to discover which will give you the sound you want. A harder pick produces a hard, biting sound. A softer pick produces a note that is softer sounding.

Using the Fingers (Fingerstyle)

Classical guitarists have always played with their fingers and in recent years many folk and some jazz guitarists have also turned to playing fingerstyle. Using your fingers allows you to pick out certain notes of the chord to create a moving melodic line as you go from chord to chord. Folk guitarists use their fingers to break the chords up into single notes for certain kinds of accompaniment patterns. Some styles have become known by the name of the artists who originated them, such as "Travis Picking," named after the great country guitarist, Merle Travis, and "Carter Picking," named after the Carter Family, well known in country music. In fingerstyle or fingerpicking, the thumb generally plays those notes that fall on the sixth, fifth, and fourth strings while the first, second, and third fingers play those notes which are on the third, second, and first strings. There are, of course, many variations of fingerings possible.

Which Style to Use

Obviously the choice of which of the above techniques to use depends on the style of music one wants to play, but I can say that it would be well to play in as many different styles as you can in order to put some variety into your playing.

Basic Theory

Note Reading

Although the major focus of this book is on chords, it would be most helpful and in some cases necessary, to be able to read notes as well.

Music notes are written on a *staff*. The staff is made up of five lines and four spaces. Each line and space represents a particular note of the musical alphabet. Placed at the beginning of each staff is a symbol called a *clef*. Guitar music uses a treble clef at the beginning of each staff.

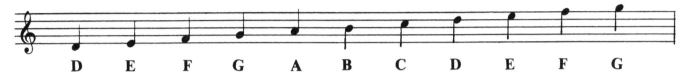

For notes that are above or below the staff, extra lines called leger lines are added.

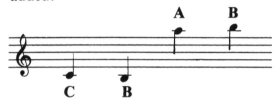

Rhythmic Notation

The way a note looks determines how long the note should be held. Below we see some of the more commonly used note values and their corresponding rests.

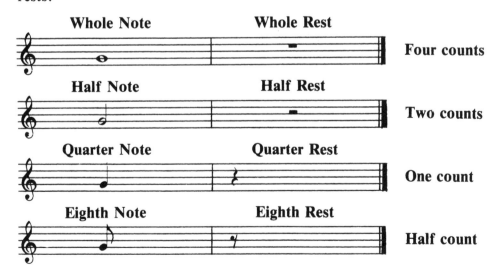

Chord Rhythm Notation

When playing rhythm guitar (chords) the notes which make up the chords are usually not written out. The chords to be played are indicated by chord symbols such as G7, C7, Fm, etc. Slanted lines called *slash* lines are used to indicate how many times to strum each chord. Below, in Figure 1, each slash line represents one beat and you strum the chord once for each beat. In Figure 2, slash lines joined by a beam (⌐⌐⌐⌐) tell you to strum each chord twice for each beat. In Figure 3, three slash lines joined by beams and with a 3 placed over or under the beam tell you to strum each cord three times for each beat.

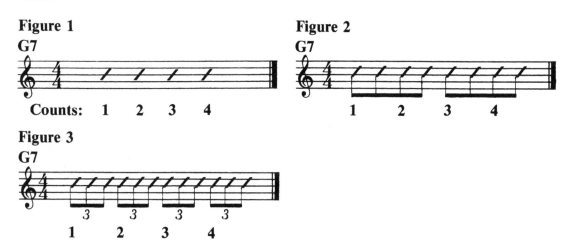

Measures and Bar Lines—Repeat Signs

Music is divided into segments called *measures*. Each measure is separated by *bar lines*. A *double bar line* indicates the end of a piece of music or a section of music. *Repeat signs* tell you to repeat a section of music.

| **Repeat sign** | **Bar line** | **Double bar line** | **Bar line** | **Repeat sign** |

Time Signatures

At the beginning of each staff is the *time signature* which tells how to count the music.

4 indicates that there are four counts in every measure.

4 indicates that the quarter note (♩) receives one count.

3 indicates that there are three counts in every measure.

4 indicates that the quarter note receives one count.

C stands for Common Time which is the same as 4/4 time.

Sharps—Flats—Naturals

1. A sharp (#) raises a note a half step (see Appendix).
2. A flat (b) lowers a note a half step.
3. A double sharp (##) or (x) raises a note a whole step.
4. A double flat (bb) lowers a note a whole step.
5. A natural (♮) cancels a previous sharp or flat.

Keys

A group of notes (or chords) all related to one common tone (or chord).

Key of C, all notes are related to the note C. C is called the key note.

Scales

A scale consists of the notes of a key placed in alphabetical order beginning and ending on the key note.

C major scale

Key Signatures

Sharps or flats placed at the beginning of a staff to indicate the key the music is written in.

Key signature for G major. **All F's are played F#**

Key signature of F major. **All B's are played Bb**

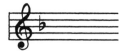

Basic Chord Theory

A chord is three or more notes played *at the same time*. The notes which make up a chord are taken from a scale. For now we will use a simple formula to make up our chords.

The major chord is formed from the first, third, and fifth notes of the major scale.

Each note in a chord has a way of being identified besides its letter name. For example, the first note of a chord is called the *root* or *tonic*. The root is the letter name of the chord. The note above the root is called the third since it is three steps up the scale. The note above the third is called the fifth since it is five steps up the scale.

A chord which contains just a root, third, and fifth is called a *triad*.

The order of the notes in a chord may be changed (these are called inversions), but their identity remains the same.

Any note in a triad may be doubled or even tripled but the chord is still a triad because it still only contains the root, third, and fifth.

Reading Chord Diagrams

Diagrams are used to show where to place the fingers of the left hand on the fingerboard. The diagrams represent a small illustration of the upper part of the guitar fingerboard. Reading these diagrams is very important.

1. The vertical lines represent the strings.

2. The horizontal lines represent the frets.

3. The numbers *on* the diagram indicate which fingers to use.

4. The numbers *under* the diagram indicate the root, third or fifth of the chord.

5. The X tells you to either mute the string (touch it lightly to deaden the sound) or to not play that string.

6. O indicates an open string and should be strummed although the string is not fingered.

7. The letter above the diagram tells you the letter name of the chord. It is called the *chord symbol.*

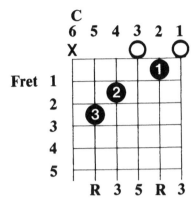

Notice that the chord has two roots and two thirds.

Open String Major Chords

Open string chords are chords that contain one or more open strings as shown in the above diagram. These are the simplest chords to play and so are usually the first chords that a guitarist learns. Most folk and blues guitarists use the open string chords and many guitar players have spent their whole careers just playing open string chords.

The diagrams illustrate the most commonly used open string chords. Notice that more than one fingering is given for the C and G chords. Practice each of the fingerings and commit them to memory.

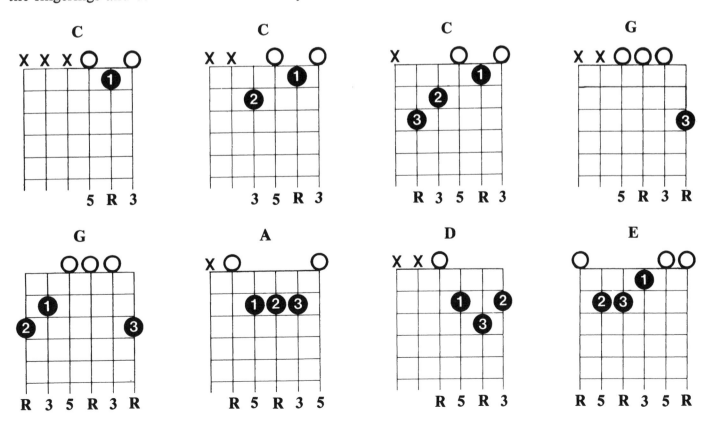

Open String Minor Chords

Minor chords are formed from the first, flatted third and fifth notes of the
major scale. A flatted note is a note lowered by a half step. (See Appendix.)
The symbol for the minor chord is the letter name of the chord and a small m.
The number of open string minor chords is limited.

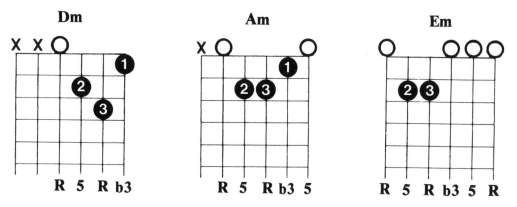

Open String Seventh Chords

The seventh chords are four note chords made up from the first, third, fifth
and flatted seventh notes of the major scale. The chords shown below are
dominant seventh chords, but the word dominant is omitted in the chord
symbol.

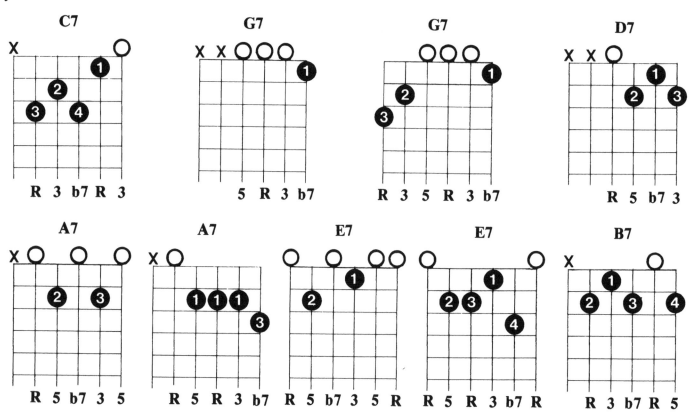

Chord Progressions

A chord progression is a series or sequence of chords which move in a forward motion. Certain progressions occur over and over again in the same song and many songs contain the same or similar progressions. The following studies are based on some of the more widely used progressions.

Progression Number 1

This first study is actually a series of short progressions made up of just two chords, the dominant seventh to the major chord. Each progression should be repeated until you can move from chord to chord smoothly and without any hesitation. All chord fingerings are shown on page 12. Use the easier fingerings to start with, then move on to the more difficult ones. Remember to strum each chord four times as indicated by the four slash lines in each measure.

Progression Number 2

Progression Number 2 consists of three chords and is given in four different keys. Again, repeat each progression until the chord changes can be made without hesitation. Refer to page 12 for chord fingerings.

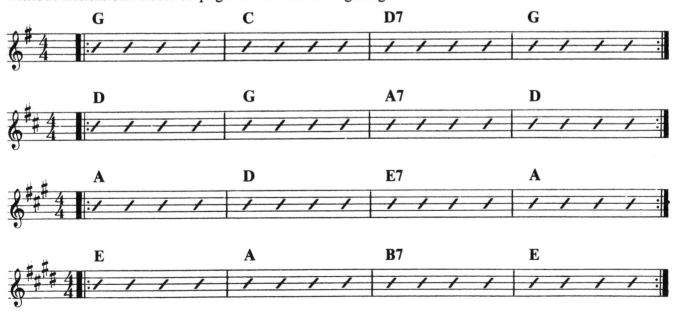

Progression Number 3

This progression is very often found in popular tunes and many of the great standards.

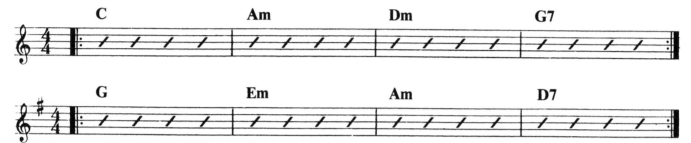

Progression Number 4

A progression in the minor key.

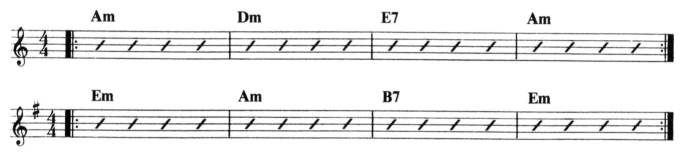

Progression Number 5

This progression is heard in many popular folk tunes.

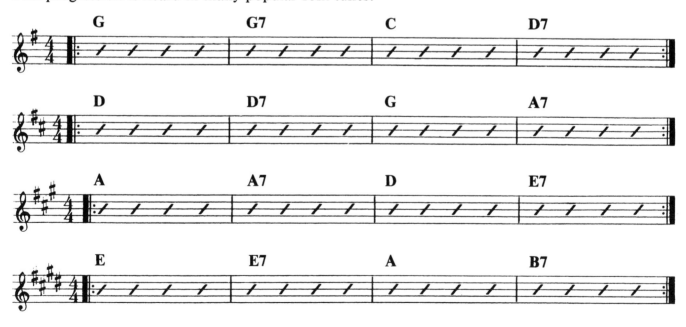

Progression Number 6

Notice that the following progression is played in 3/4 time, meaning that you will strike each chord three times in each measure.

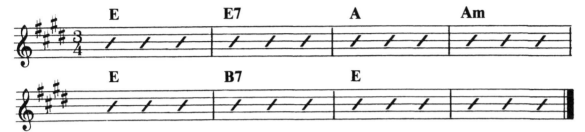

Basic Accompaniments

At this point you should be quite comfortable playing all of the chords given so far. Now let's learn some basic accompaniment patterns.

Root-Chord

The first accompaniment pattern is the *root-chord* pattern. The root of the chord is played (with either thumb or pick) on the first beat of the measure. The rest of the notes of the chord are played on each of the remaining beats of the measure. Below are two ways in which this might be notated musically.

Pattern in the key of C with the notes written out:

With the roots indicated and slashes to indicate chords:

In 3/4 time the pattern would be:

The same pattern in the key of G:

In 3/4 time:

Alternating Bass

Another accompaniment which is less monotonous than the root–chord pattern is one which uses an *alternating bass*. The alternate bass note is usually the fifth of the chord. In some cases it may be the third.

In 3/4 time:

The same pattern in the key of G:

In 3/4 time:

Fingerstyle

A very pleasant sounding accompaniment can be performed by playing chords with the fingers of the right hand. This is referred to as *fingerstyle*. Place your right hand in position over the sound hole with the fingers curved slightly inward. Place the thumb on the lowest note of the chord you are about to play. Place the fingertip of the first finger (the part between the nail and the flesh of the finger) on the underside of the third string, the fingertip of the second finger on the underside of the second string and the fingertip of the third finger on the underside of the first string. With these fingers resting lightly and comfortably on the underside of the first three strings, strike the root note with your thumb and then pluck the strings, simultaneously moving the three fingers inward toward the palm in a gentle, plucking manner. Move the fingers evenly so that they sound together. Play the examples given above using fingerstyle.

Arpeggio Accompaniments

Another very effective accompaniment is the *arpeggio accompaniment*. This is produced by playing the chord one note at a time rather than all at once as you have been doing. Place your hand in postition for fingerstyle but instead of plucking all the notes simultaneously, play each note separately. The thumb plays the bass note, the first finger plays the note on the third string, the second finger plays the note on the second string and the third finger plays the note on the first string. The following examples illustrate a few of the many ways of playing these arpeggiated accompaniment patterns.

Note: that when using the alternating bass on the dominant seventh chord, the fifth is very often played first and the root is played as the alternate bass note. This is a widely used practice. It is important not to rush the notes of the arpeggio. Play evenly and count carefully.

Connecting Chords with Bass Runs

To add interest to a series of chords a device called a *bass run* may be used. Bass runs are single note passages that lead you out of one chord and into the next.

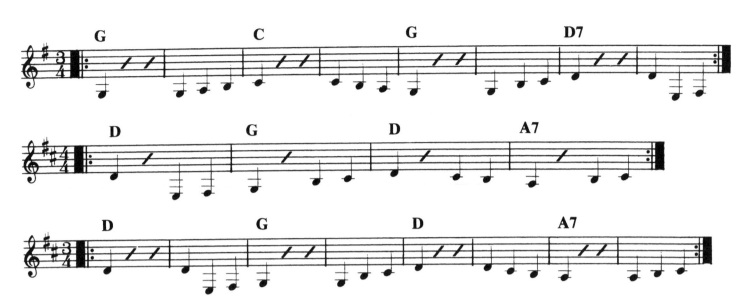

This next progression contains our first non-open string chord. It is the F major chord. Notice that the first finger is used to cover two strings. With practice this should not be too difficult.

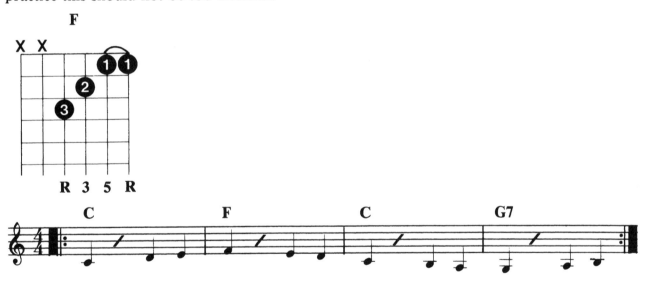

In 3/4 time:

Here are more examples of bass runs in different keys in 4/4 time and 3/4 time.

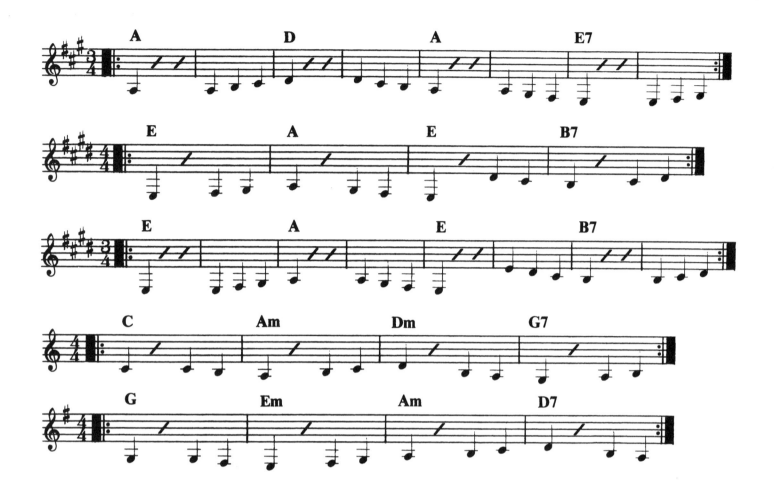

Barre Chords

The chords most favored by rock guitarists are the barre chords. The barre chord is a chord in which one finger covers three or more strings and there are no open strings. The diagrams below illustrate the basic barre chord forms. For purposes of identification we will label these forms as Form One.

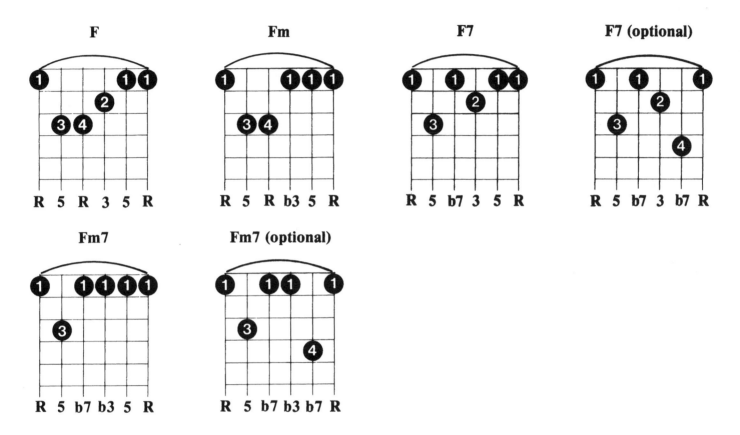

The following exercise is based on the barre chords played up the fingerboard starting from the first fret up to the twelfth fret. Play the exercise four times, first as major chords, then minor chords, then seventh chords and finally as minor seventh chords. It is important that you memorize the name of the chord played at each fret.

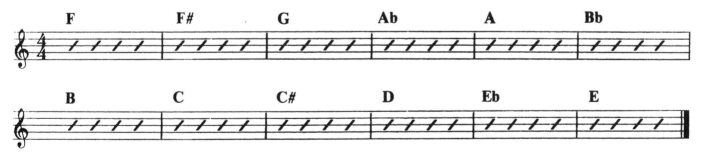

Below are the Form Two barre chords. The root of each of these chords is the note played on the fifth string.

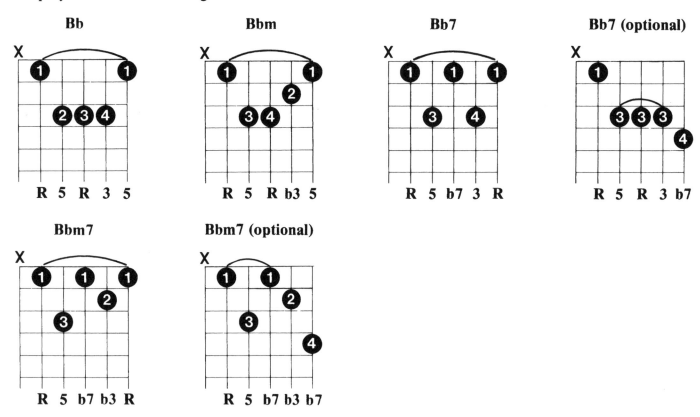

The following exercise shows the name of the chord played at each fret starting from the first fret. Play the exercise four times using each of the four chord qualities.

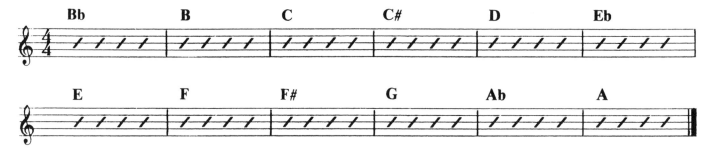

Combining Barre Chord Forms

The following exercise shows you the two possible chords played at each fret. For example, at the first fret, if you play the Form One fingerings you will produce the F, the Fm, the F7 and the Fm7 chords. If you play the Form Two fingerings at the first fret you will produce the Bb, the Bbm, the Bb7 and the Bbm7 chords. The exercise moves up the fingerboard one fret at a time. The numbers indicate which form to use. Play the exercise using the four qualities of chords.

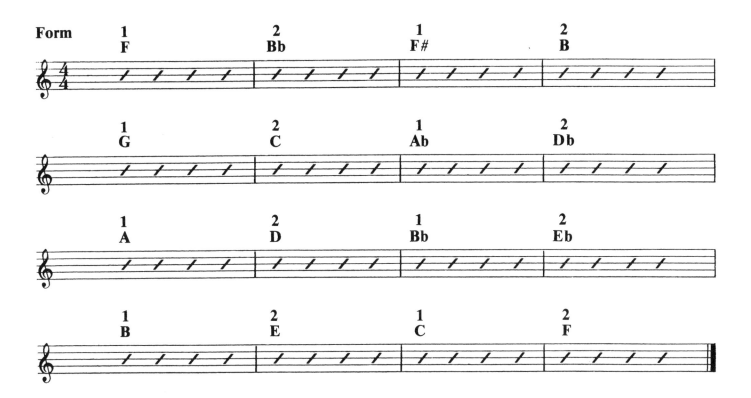

In the following exercise the numbers are omitted. A good general rule
to follow in deciding which chord form to use is to use the form closest to the
chord you are already playing.

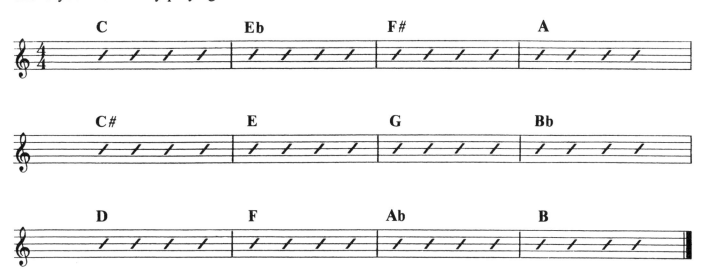

The following exercise is based on the most widely used progression in all of music. The progression is just two measures long and the exercise takes us through all the major keys. We will have a thorough study of progressions later but for now we are just trying to develop facility in playing chords all over the fingerboard. Avoid making jumps from chord to chord. Always play the chord form closest to the one you are playing.

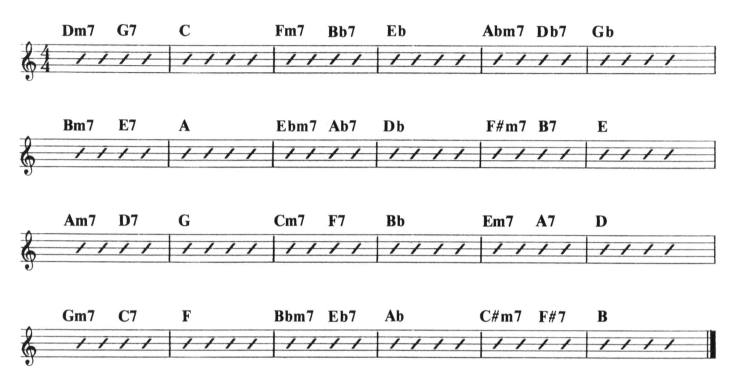

Here is another two measure progression used in many popular tunes. The progression is given through all the major keys.

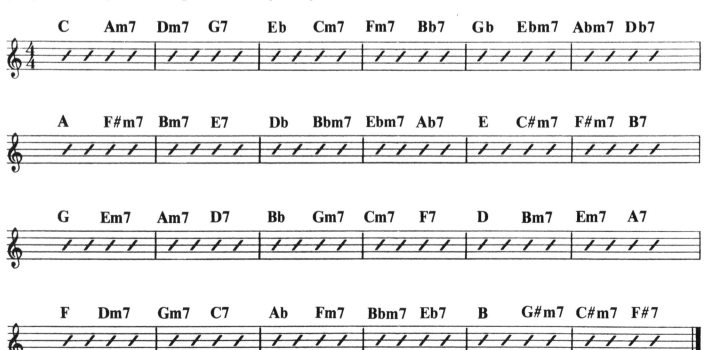

Accompaniment Patterns

The following accompaniment patterns are used with rock type progressions.
All patterns should be played with a pick. ⊓ means to strum down and ∨
means to strum up. Repeat each pattern until you can play it smoothly and feel
comfortable with it.

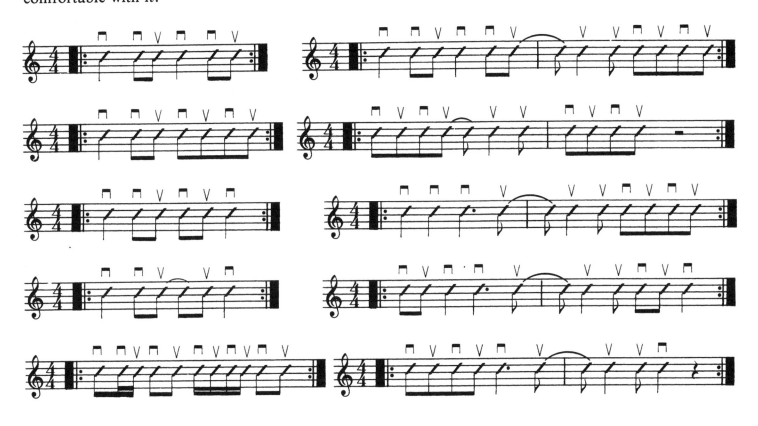

These next accompaniment patterns use single bass notes followed by the full
barre chord. The patterns are most effective when playing a slow tune when
you want the accompaniment to sound full. Use a G7 Form One barre chord.

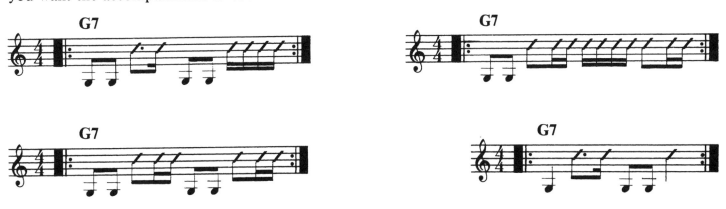

Barre Chord Variations

The following barre chord forms are derived from the basic forms you've just learned. Some are difficult to finger but as you play up the fingerboard where the frets are narrower they become easier to play.

Form One Variations

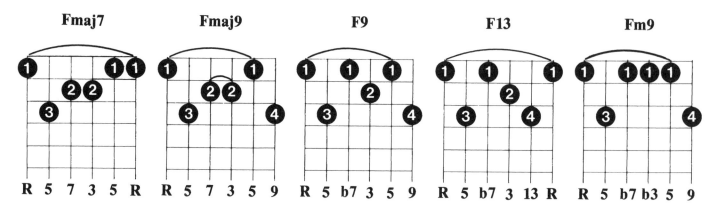

Form Two Variations

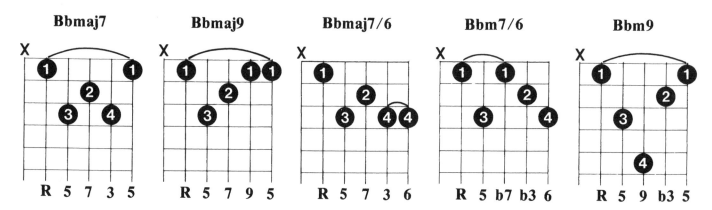

Blues Progressions

One of the most widely used progressions by all rock and jazz bands is the blues progression. Below are two versions of the blues. The first is favored by most rock bands and the second by bands who are more into jazz. Even more advanced progressions will be given later.

Progression Number 1

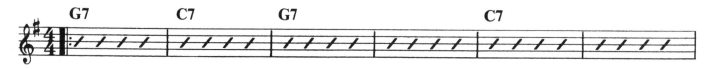

Progression Number 2

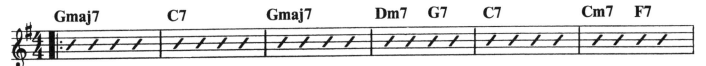

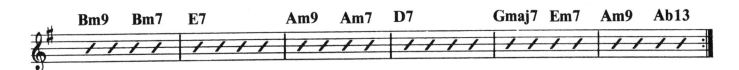

A Rock Pattern

A very popular effect, particularly in the blues, is illustrated below. First practice the chord movement going from the seventh chord to the seventh (add 6) chord.

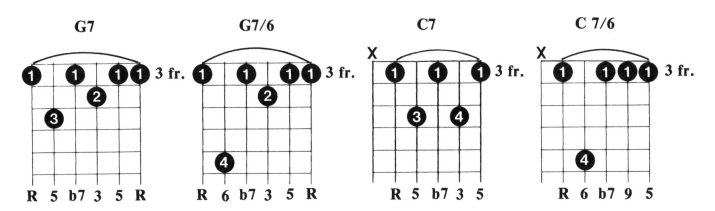

Having practiced the chord movement, play the following rhythmic pattern. Bring out the moving line on the fifth string when playing the G7 chords and the moving line on the fourth string when playing the C7 chords.

Very often the above pattern is played by sounding just the two notes which make up the melodic line.

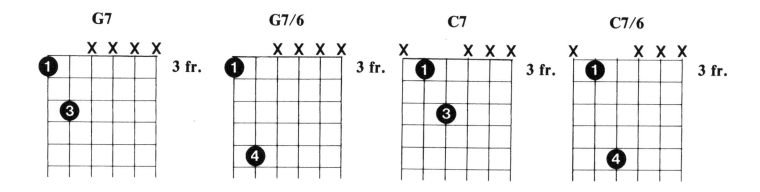

Here is the musical notation for the above pattern. Notice that it might be easier to play the C chords up at the eighth fret.

Jazz Chords

Jazz players rarely use barre chord forms because the placing of the first finger across all six strings is too restrictive and doesn't allow for much flexibility. It limits the kind of chords that can be played. Also, barre chords contain many doubled and even tripled notes and rather than doubling a note a jazz guitarist prefers using another color tone.

We'll begin our study of jazz chords with the most commonly used forms. All of the following chords have their root on the sixth string. It is very important that you memorize the relative position of each note within the chord. For example, you should know that the note played on the third string is the third of the chord, the note played on the second string is the fifth of the chord, etc.

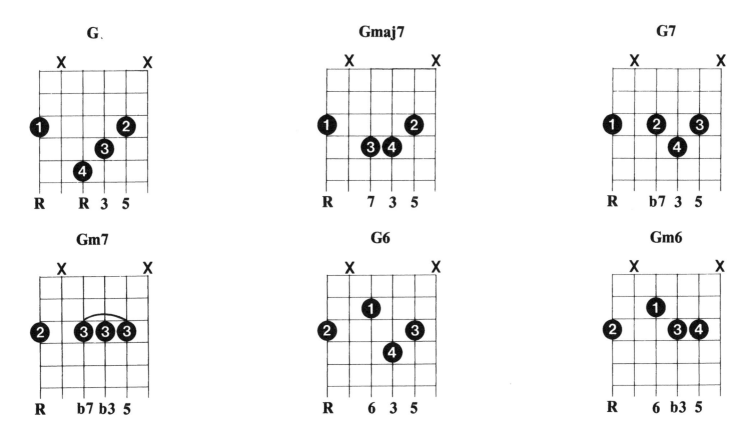

Note: although the G major chord is shown above it is rarely used. It is included to show how the other chords derive from it.

The following fingerboard diagram shows the letter name of each chord at each fret on the sixth string. Practice the above chord forms up the fingerboard.

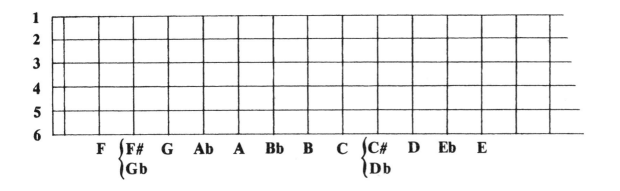

After playing the chords up the fingerboard and learning the name of each chord at each fret the following exercise will help develop facility.

Play the exercise six times: as major chords, as major sevenths, as dominant sevenths, as minor sevenths, as major sixths, and finally as minor sixths. When playing the F6 and Fm6 at the first fret you will have to play the open fourth string.

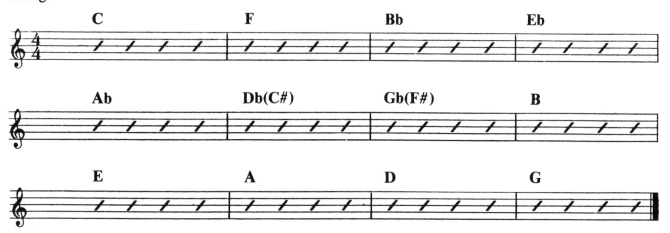

Alternate Chord Forms

Another form of chords which have their root on the sixth string are shown below. These are less practical than those you've just learned because they are harder to play, sound muddier and are more difficult to alter and extend. However you should know them.

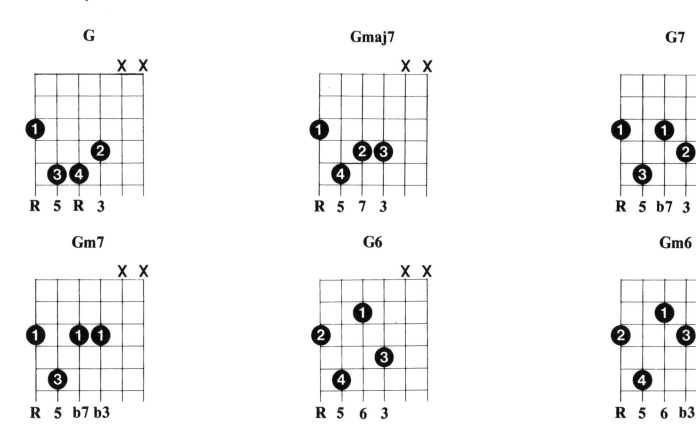

These forms will be dealt with later when we discuss harmonized scales, so if you wish to wait until that point you may do so.

A Typical Standard Progression

The following study is based on chords which are typical of many standard tunes of the 1930s and 1940s. For example, the song "Blue Moon" would fit very well over these chords. All chords have their root on the sixth string and the forms are all taken from the chords shown on page 29.

Note: some chord forms have more than one possible name. For example, G6 is also Em7 and Am6 is also D9. We will learn more about this as we progress. For now I have chosen to call the chord by the letter name that the student is most familiar with at this time.

Inversions

All of the jazz chords learned so far have their root in the bass (the lowest string). These chords are said to be in *root position*. When a note other than the root is in the bass the chord is said to be inverted. Below we see all the inversions of a Cmaj7 chord.

Cmaj7

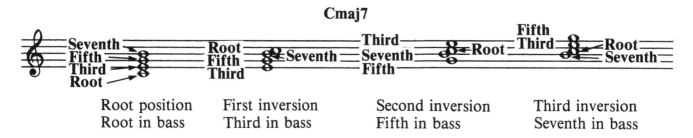

| Root position | First inversion | Second inversion | Third inversion |
| Root in bass | Third in bass | Fifth in bass | Seventh in bass |

The following chord diagrams illustrate the basic chord forms and inversions of the chords you have learned so far.

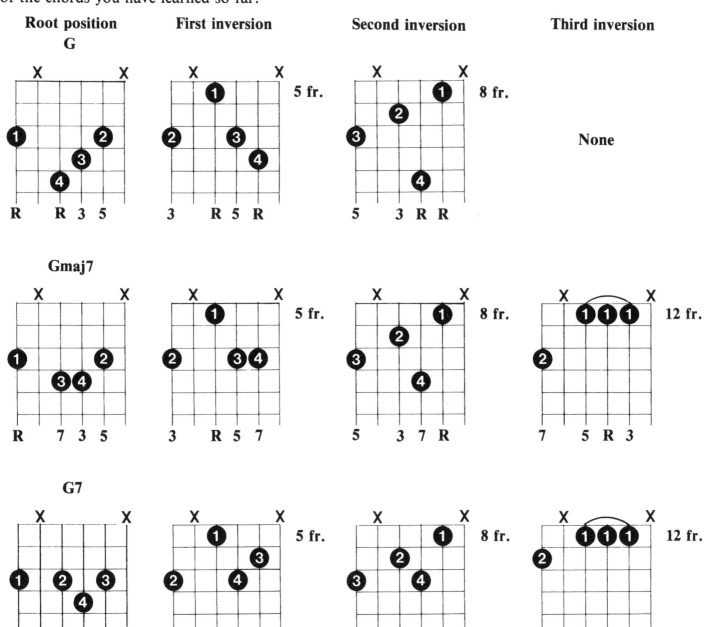

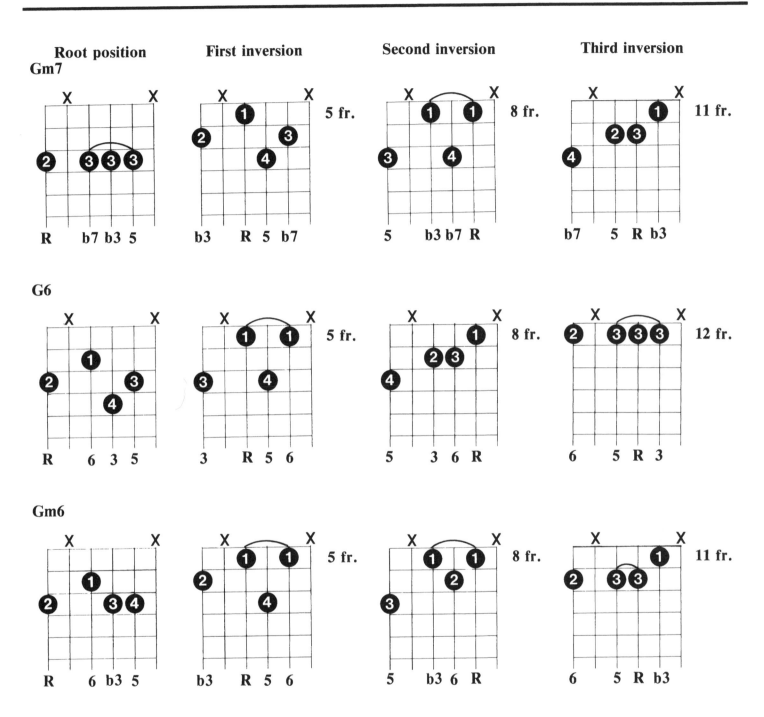

Inverted Chord Drills

Play the following exercise. The letter or number above each chord symbol indicates which note is played in the bass.

R	3	5	R	3	5	7	R
C	C	C	Cmaj7	Cmaj7	Cmaj7	Cmaj7	C7

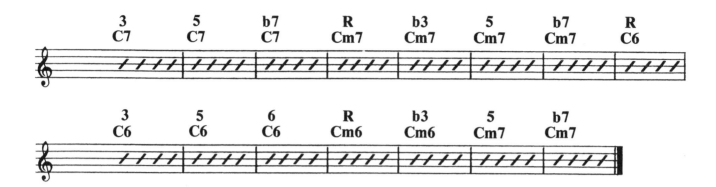

Now that you have completed the above exercise do the same with the following chords: F, Bb, Eb, Ab, Db, Gb, B, E, A, D, and G. Although this is a tedious exercise it will be well worth the time spent in doing it.

Choosing the Correct Inversion

One of the advantages of knowing the different chord inversions is that you don't have to jump all over the fingerboard in going from chord to chord. You simply go to the nearest chord inversion. For example: if you are playing a Gmaj7 chord and the next chord is an Em7, instead of playing the Gmaj7 at the third fret and the Em7 at the twelfth fret, just play the Em7 with the third in the bass and you can stay at the third fret.

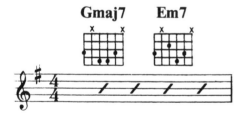

The third of Em7 is G. G is also the root of the Gmaj7 chord. Look back to page 31. In the first measure the G6 is the given chord symbol, the correct chord is Em7 but at that point you did not know the inversions. The fingering for a G6 (root in the bass) is the *same* as the Em7 third in the bass. Both chords contain exactly the same notes.

Suppose you are playing a Gm7 chord and the next chord is C7. The note G is the root of the Gm7 chord and is also the fifth of the C7. Therefore you play the C7 with the fifth in the bass.

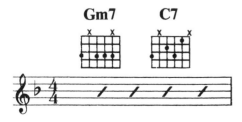

If you are playing a Gm7 chord with the flatted third in the bass followed by a C7 chord, the note Bb is the flatted third of Gm7 and is also the flatted seventh of C7. Therefore, play the C7 with the flatted seventh in the bass.

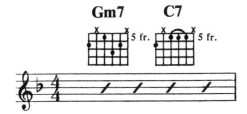

Now take a progression that you've worked on before. Here are some of the different ways you could play it using the chords you have just learned. The important things to look for are *common tones*, that is, notes that are in the same chord and notes that are *near* to those in the chord you are coming from.

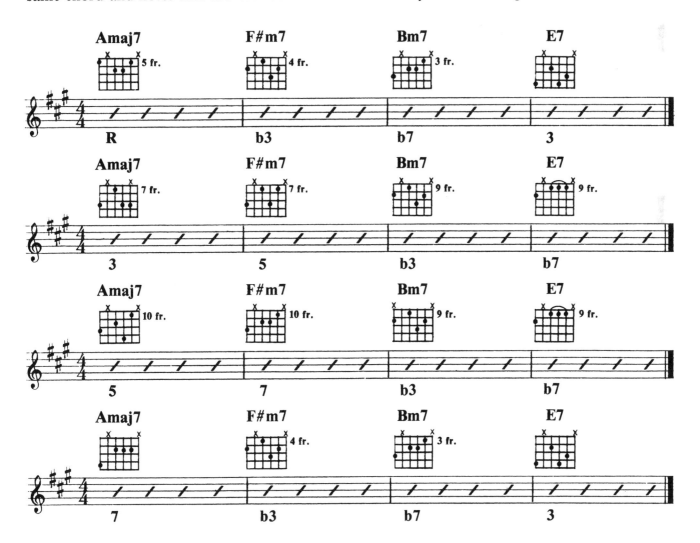

Here is another progression familiar to you, with four different ways of playing it using the various inversions.

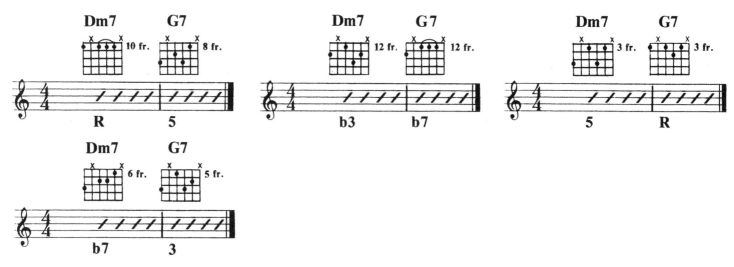

This progression as well as the progression on page 35 should be played in as many different keys as you can.

After playing the above progression and the one on page 35 it should be obvious that some chord forms sound better with certain notes in the bass than with other bass notes. As a general rule, the chord forms with the root in the bass are the best sounding, the fifth in the bass the next best, and thirds and sevenths are the weakest sounding. Chords with thirds or sevenths in the bass are best used as passing chords, that is, to pass between two chords in order to create a more interesting bass line. The following examples will illustrate this.

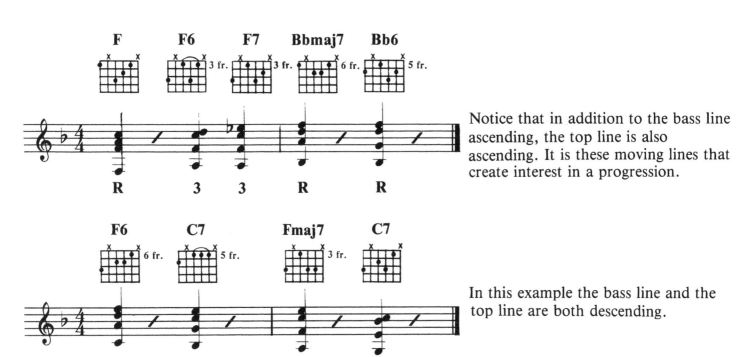

Notice that in addition to the bass line ascending, the top line is also ascending. It is these moving lines that create interest in a progression.

In this example the bass line and the top line are both descending.

As we learn more chord forms we will see more examples of good moving lines.

"*Rhythm*" *Study*

The following study is based on the chords to a song much favored by jazz musicians, "I Got Rhythm." Later we will explore some ways to make it sound more interesting but for now concentrate on moving from chord to chord in as smooth a manner as possible. Look for common tones and close chord forms.

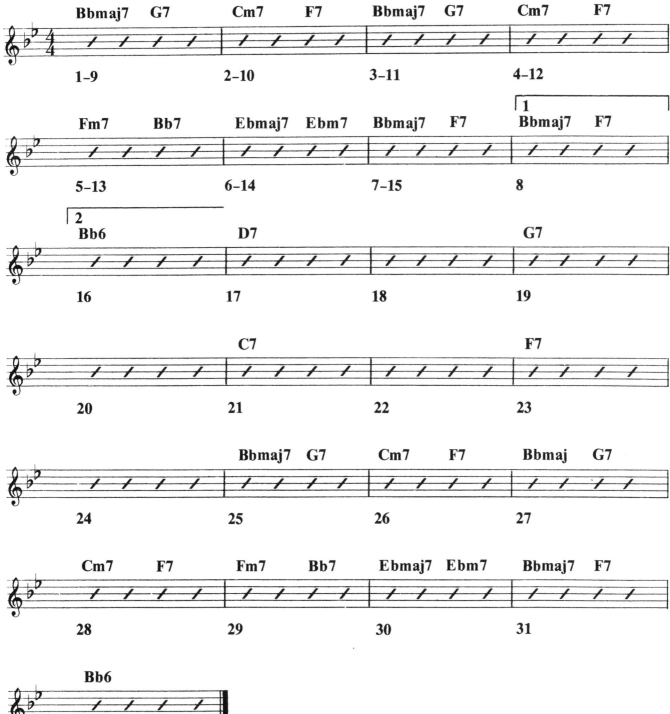

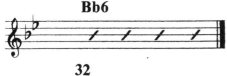

A Standard Popular Tune

Here are the chords to another popular standard. Chord diagrams are given showing one possible way of playing the chords. Notice that the bass notes are also shown. As you learn more chord forms more possibilities will become available.

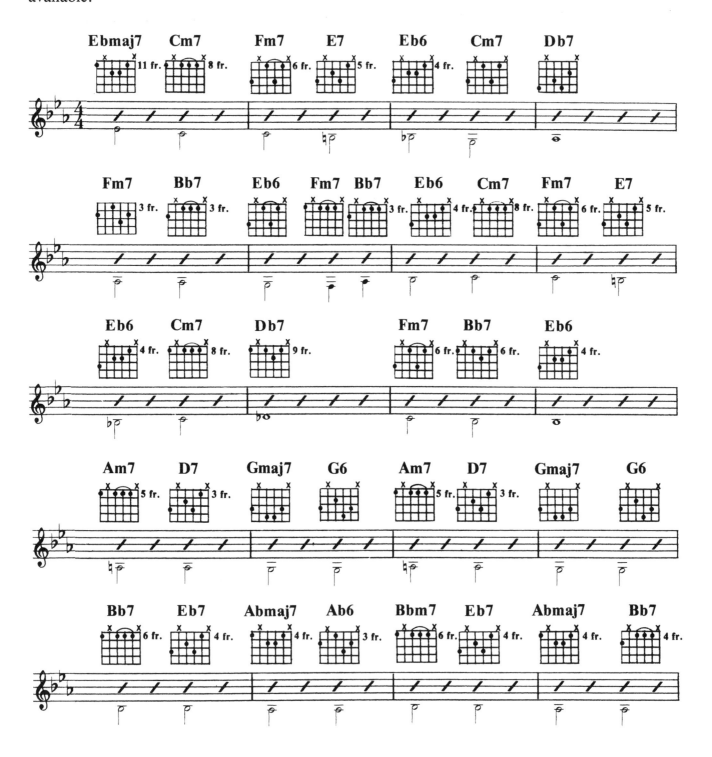

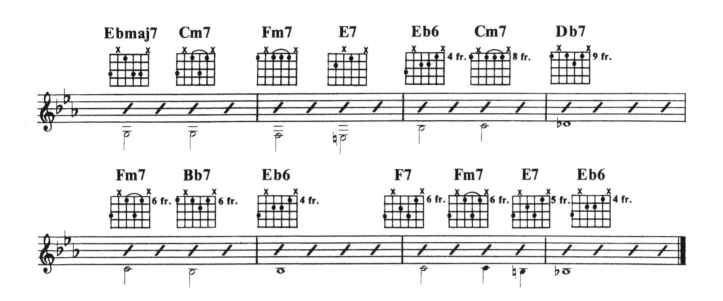

Where Chords and Progressions Come From

Now that we've gone through a variety of chords it's time that we took a closer look at where chords and progressions come from. The following is a brief discussion of the three basic elements which make up music. Melody, harmony, and rhythm.

Melody

A melody is simply a sequence of single tones, the tune of a particular song. Anytime you hum or whistle anything you are humming or whistling a *melody*. The notes which make up a melody come from what we call a key. A key is a group of tones which are all related to one common tone. This common tone is called the *tonic* or *keynote*. This is the tone that all other tones in the key move toward. It is the note that usually ends a song. If you are playing a song in the key of C, for example, all the notes of the melody will move toward, and finally end, on the note C, the tonic. The C will give the feeling of having come to a complete rest; a sense of finality. Play the following melody:

Notice how the little melody comes to rest on the tonic C. The melody is in the key of C. When the tones of the key are placed in alphabetical order starting with the tonic, we have a scale.

Scale of C major

Harmony

Harmony occurs when we sound three or more tones simultaneously, forming a chord. These chords are used to accompany a given melody. Earlier we learned that chords may be formed by following a certain mathematical formula, for example, by taking the first, third, fifth and seventh notes of a major scale we form the major seventh chord; by taking the first, third, fifth and flatted seventh notes we form the dominant seventh chord. Of course that is all correct but another way of forming chords is as follows.

For purposes of illustration we will use the key of C major but you must understand that whatever applies in the key of C holds true for all the major keys.

Below once again is the C major scale:

Chords may be built on each note of the scale by stacking notes in intervals of a third above each note of the scale. Every chord contains only the notes within the scale. The result is called the *harmonized scale.*

C Major Harmonized Scale

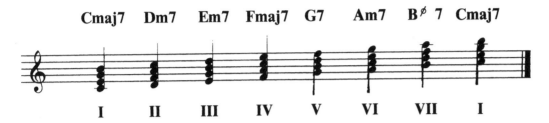

Each of the chords in the above harmonized scale is identified by its letter name and a Roman numeral. The Roman numeral identifies the position of each chord in the scale. For example, the I chord in the key of C is the Cmaj7, the V chord is the G7, etc.

In *all* major keys, the I and IV chords are major sevenths, the II, III, and VI chords are minor sevenths, the V chord is a dominant seventh and the VII chord is a half diminished seventh, sometimes called a minor seventh flatted fifth.

The major sixth chord found in many progressions is also formed from the first and fourth notes of the major scale. The sixth chord is often used with, or in place of, the major chord.

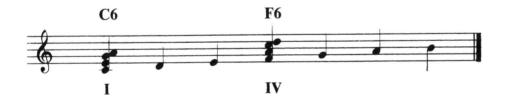

Key Areas

Most musical compositions base their melodies and harmonies on at least one, but usually more, major scales. The exception would be the compositions of the experimental composers. For our purposes we will refer to the more standard compositions found in rock, jazz and pop music. Quite often a piece will start in one key and then move through a number of different keys before coming to an end. It is important for the guitarist who functions as a rhythm player in a band to know how to identify these key changes or *key areas* so that he can choose the correct chord forms and perhaps embellish the chords to create a more interesting background.

In every key there are certain chords which establish the key. Those chords are the I chord, the II chord and the V chord. These chords are enough to indicate to the experienced musician what key a particular part of a piece is in. The chords are usually found in the order of II–V–I so that, for example, seeing Dm7–G7–Cmaj7 is enough to tell a musician that at that point the piece is in the key of C.

Here are the chords to a very popular standard tune. Although the key signature tells us that the tune is in the key of C, the chords in the first four measures are Am7–D7–Gmaj7–G6 indicating that those four measures are in the key of G. The tune moves through several keys before finally ending in C. All the key areas are bracketed. Notice that some keys are indicated by just the II–V chords.

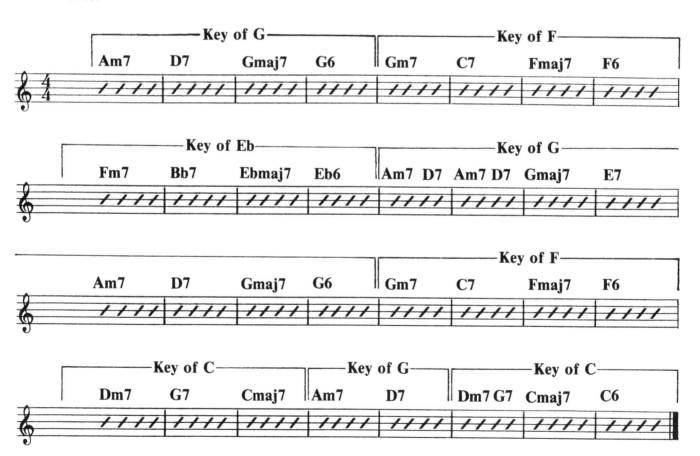

The following chord background is taken from another popular standard tune.
The various key areas are indicated by just the II–V chords. It isn't necessary
to resolve the II–V to the I chord to indicate a key area.

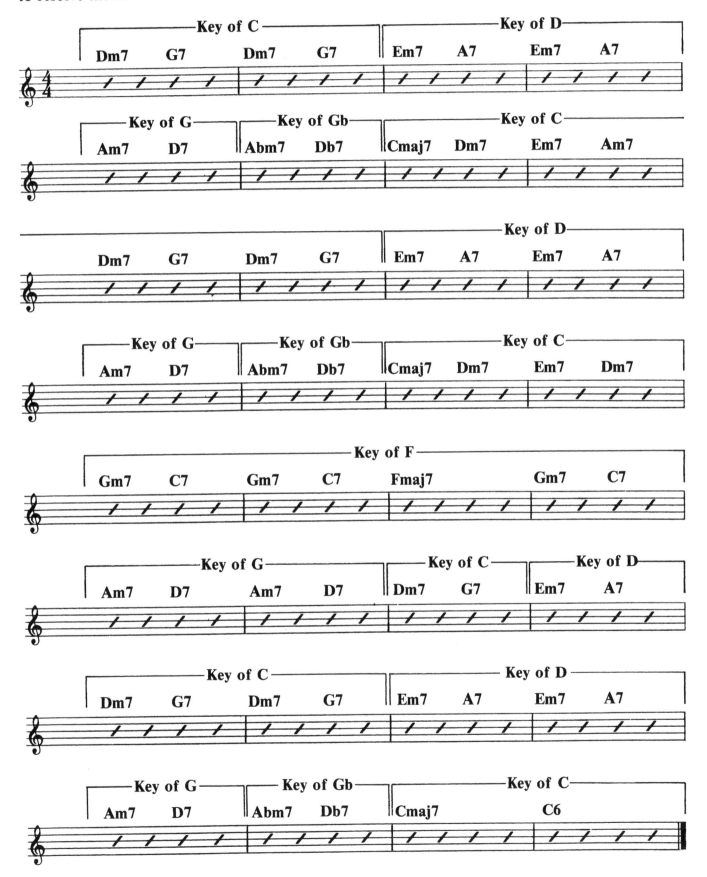

Another sequence of chords used to indicate a particular key area is the
I–VI–II–V progression. The following chordal background contains examples
of I–VI–II–V, II–V–I and II–V progressions.

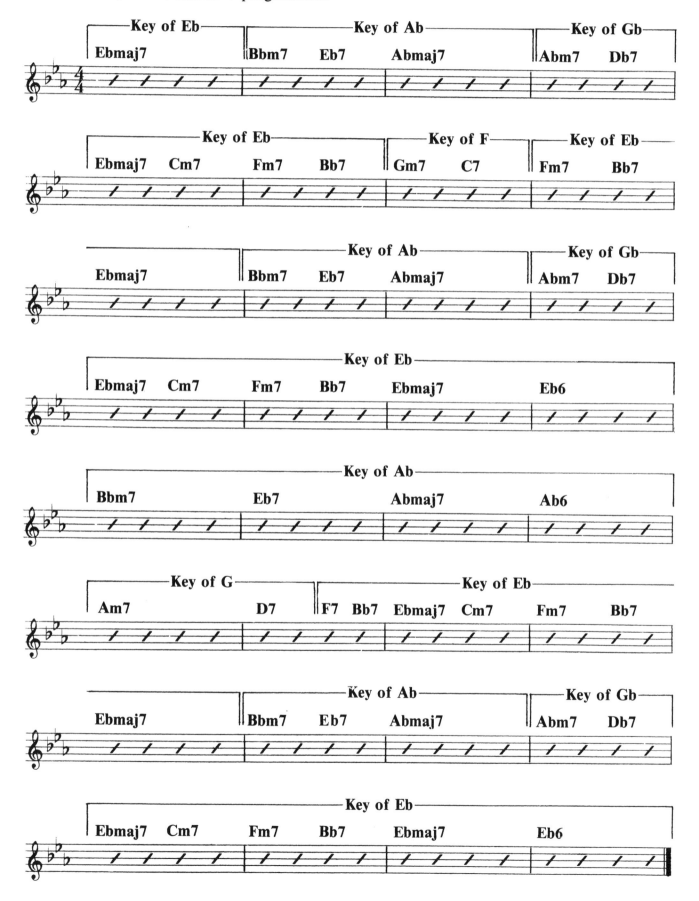

Different Chord Forms

Chords with Their Root on the Fifth String

This next series of chords is formed within the middle four strings of the guitar fingerboard. These chords have their root on the fifth string. Once again, memorize the relative position of each note on each string within the chord. For example, you should know that the root of the chord is played on the fifth string, the third of the chord is on the second string, the fifth of the chord is on the fourth string and so on.

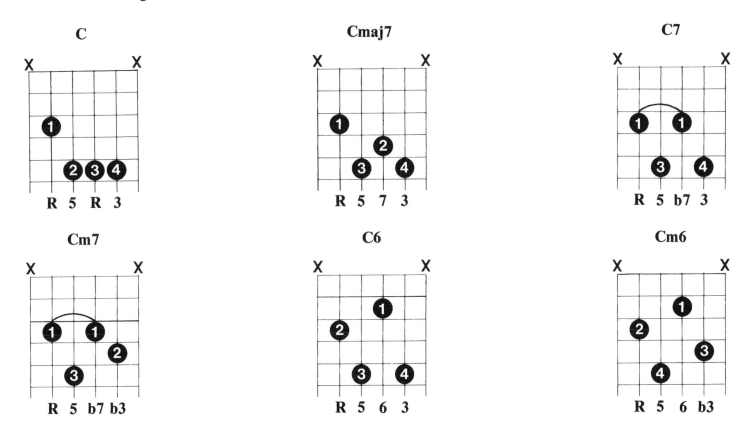

Although the major sixth chord is rather difficult to finger, with practice it can be done.

The following fingerboard diagram illustrates the letter name of each chord at each fret on the fifth string. Play each of the above chords up the fingerboard and memorize the name of each chord at each fret.

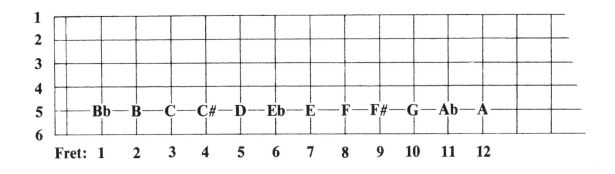

After you've played the new chord forms up the fingerboard and know the names of the chords at each fret the following exercise will help you to gain facility. Notice that only the letter name of each chord is given, play the exercise through six times for each chord quality as you did on page 30.

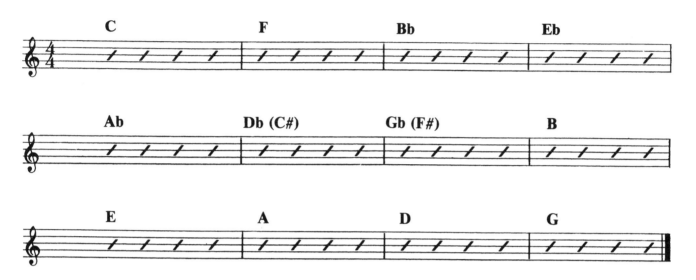

Note that the voicings for these chords with their root on the fifth string are exactly the same as those for the alternate chords with the root on the sixth string, shown on page 30.

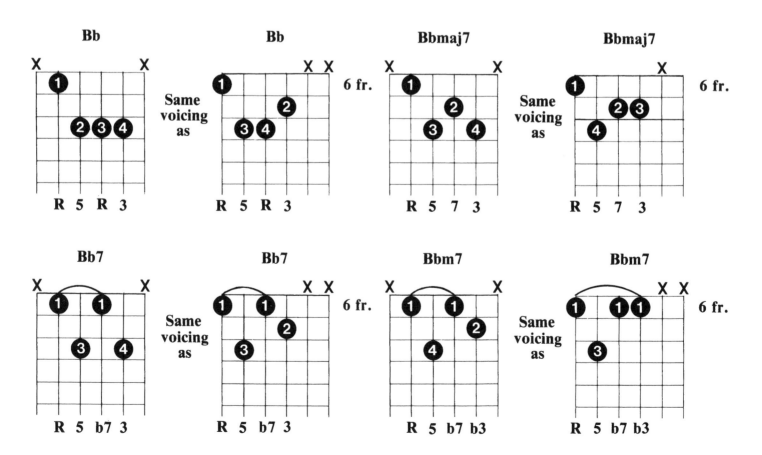

The fact that these voicings are exactly the same is important to know if you wish to have a consistent sound in a progression. You will see the significance of this later on.

Alternate Chord Forms with Their Root on the Fifth String

On page 45 we learned a set of chord forms which had their root on the fifth string. On page 46 we saw how these new chord forms are voiced exactly the same as the alternate chord forms with the root on the sixth string, shown on page 30. Here are an alternate set of chord forms for those chords whose root is on the fifth string but whose voicings are a little more open than those shown on page 46.

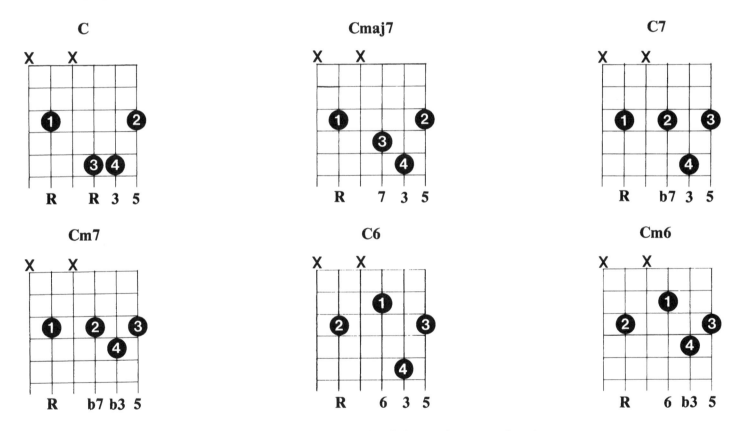

Below we see how some of the more commonly used of these alternate chord forms have exactly the same voicings as the chord forms with the root on the sixth string shown on page 29.

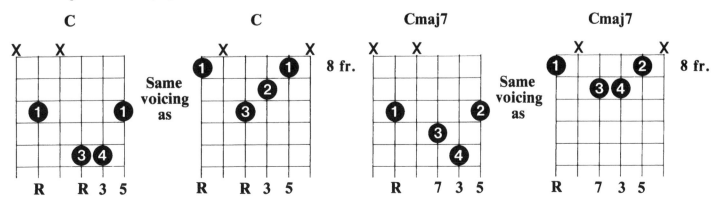

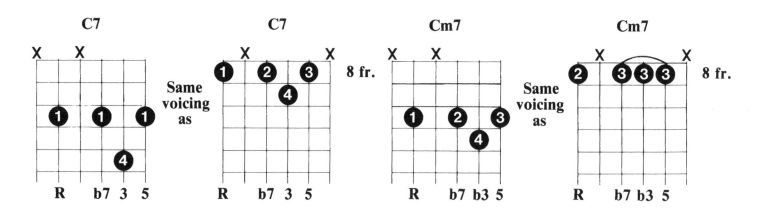

Combining Chords with Their Root on the Fifth and Sixth Strings

The following exercise is based on a series of II–V–I chords in all the major keys. By using chords whose root is on the sixth string and those whose root is on the fifth string it is possible to keep all roots in the bass which is sometimes very desirable, particularly when playing without a bass player. Beneath each measure a five or six indicates on which string the root is to be played. Although the major sixth chords are included, omit them if they are still too difficult.

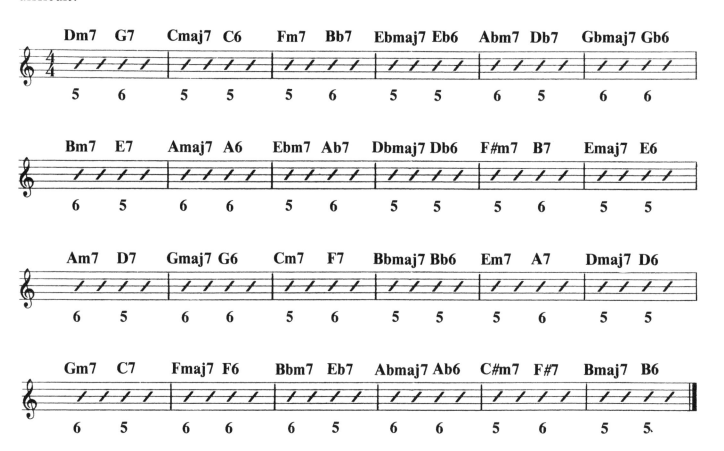

When playing F6 with the root on the sixth string or Bb6 with the root on the fifth string you will have to play an open string. The fourth string will be open for the F6 and the third string for the Bb6.

More Chords with Their Root on the Fifth String

Here are several more chord forms which have their root on the fifth string. Note that these forms also have their root on the second string and that the fifth of the chord is omitted. If you look back to pages 32 and 33, those chord forms which have the fifth in the bass, you will notice the similarity of the chord forms. Any chord form which has its fifth on the sixth string will have its root on the second string.

C7

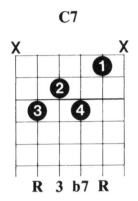

R 3 b7 R

C6

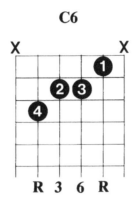

R 3 6 R

Cm7

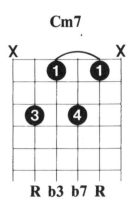

R b3 b7 R

The following fingerboard diagram illustrates the letter name of each chord at each fret on the fifth string. Play the above chord forms up the fingerboard and memorize the name of the chord at each fret.

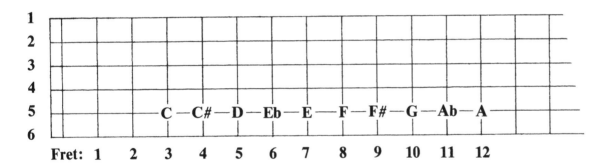

Here are several examples of the use of the above chord forms:

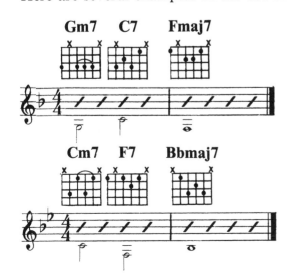

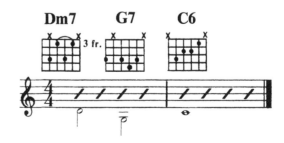

As you increase your knowledge of chord forms the greater the confusion can be as to which forms to use. Earlier in the book we learned some good general rules to follow and it would be good to review them at this time. Use forms which have common tones so that you don't have to move your hand too much. Use forms which lay close to each other and avoid jumping all over the fingerboard.

Below are the chords to the same popular standard tune as shown on page 38. The chord diagrams show another possible accompaniment which includes the chord forms just learned. Note the greater use of root chord forms. This type of accompaniment is best when there is no bass player to supply the roots.

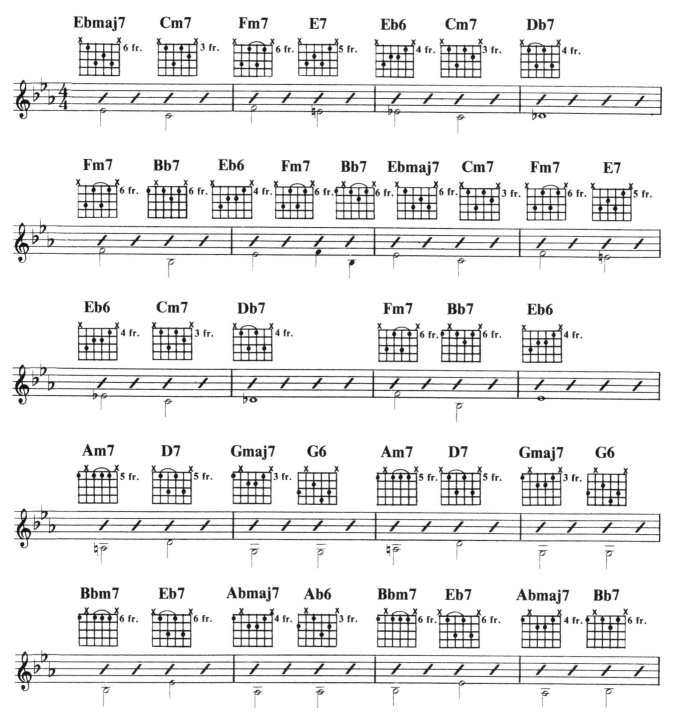

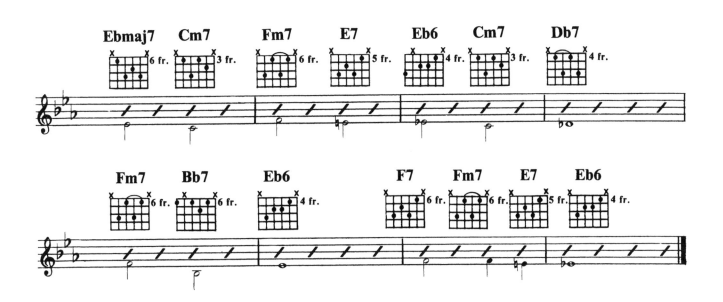

Extended and Altered Chords

In the early 1940s a new era in jazz began to emerge. It came to be called bebop or more simply bop. Some of its leading innovators were Charlie Parker, Dizzy Gillespie and Thelonious Monk. One of the important innovations which came out of this new jazz style was in the area of harmony. Chords were extended and notes within the chords were altered to create more interest and color. The chords which were most affected by these new harmonic innovations were the I chord, the II chord and the V chord.

The I Chord

The I chord (the major seventh) was extended to the major ninth. To the major ninth was added the sixth. The diagrams below illustrate some of the more commonly used major type chords.

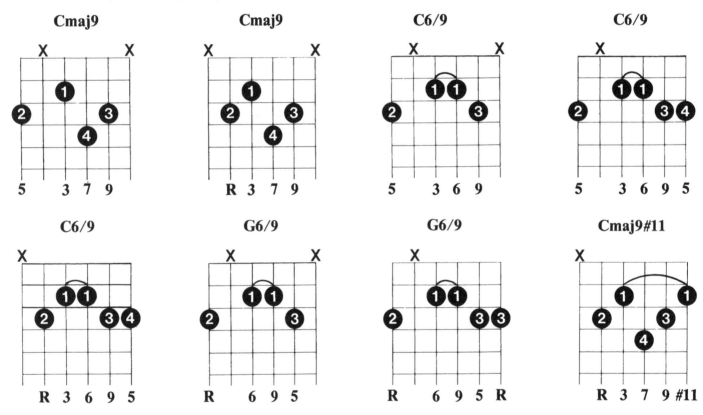

The II Chord

The II chord (the minor seventh) was extended to a ninth or an eleventh. The fifth of the chord was sometimes altered to a flatted fifth.

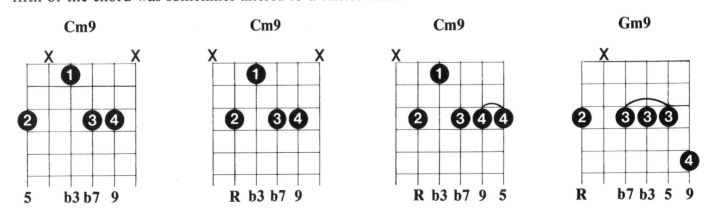

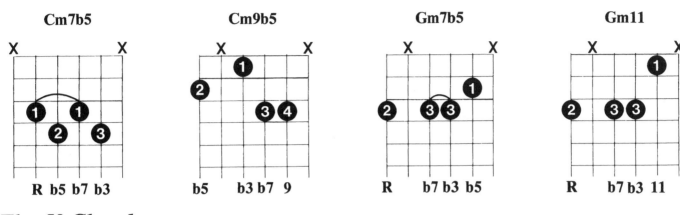

The V Chord

The V chord (the dominant seventh) was the chord offering the most possible extensions and alterations. Below are some of the more widely used of these chords. Memorize all of the forms for the V chords, and also the I and II chords, and play them all over the fingerboard.

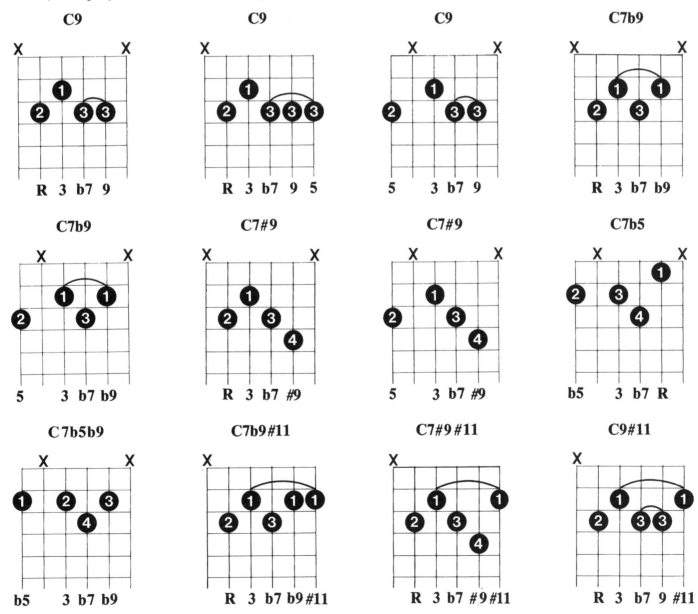

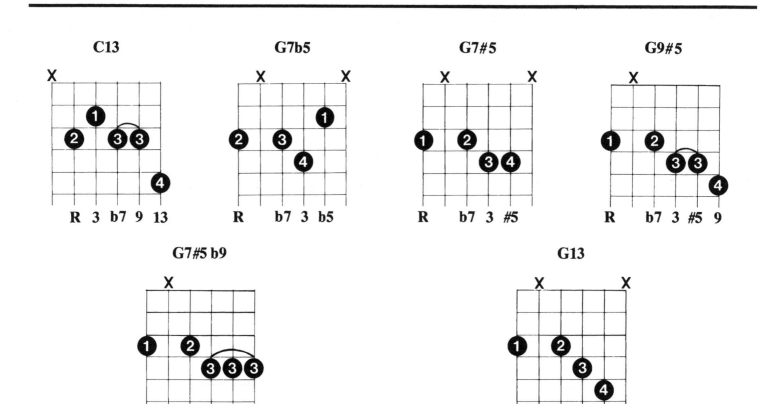

C13

X

R 3 b7 9 13

G7b5

X X

R b7 3 b5

G7#5

X X

R b7 3 #5

G9#5

X

R b7 3 #5 9

G7#5 b9

X

R b7 3 #5 b9

G13

X X

R b7 3 13

Chord Embellishments

The new chord forms you have just learned are used to add color and interest to the bland, basic chords found in most tunes. The table below lists the basic chords and the chords which may be used in their place.

Table of Chord Embellishments

(Key of C major)

Basic Chord	Embellishment
I chord (C or Cmaj7)	C6, Cmaj9, C6/9, Cmaj9#11
II chord (Dm7)	Dm9, Dm7b5, Dm11
V chord (G7)	G9, G7b9, G7#9, G7b5, G7#5, G7b5b9, G7b9#11, G7#9#11, G9#5, G7#5b9, G9#11, G13

The following examples will illustrate how some of these chords may be used to embellish a basic II–V–I progression. In addition to the chord diagrams, the bass note and the top note of each chord are given so that you can see as well as hear how these "voices" move. All examples should be played in other keys all over the fingerboard.

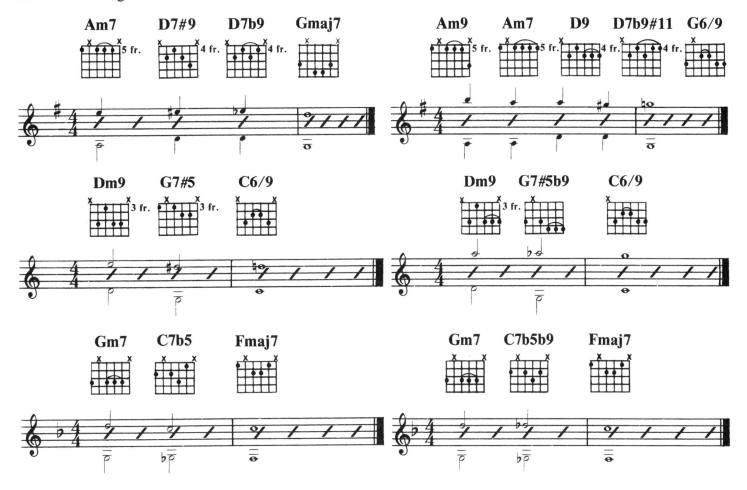

The following examples are based on the I–VI–II–V progression.

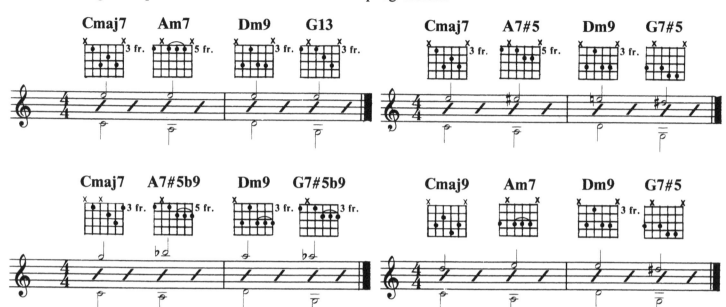

Note how careful use of extended and altered chords helps to create interesting melodic lines in the top voices of the progressions.

A Standard Popular Tune with Chord Embellishments

Here again is the standard popular tune shown on page 38. This chord background makes use of some of the chord embellishments just learned.

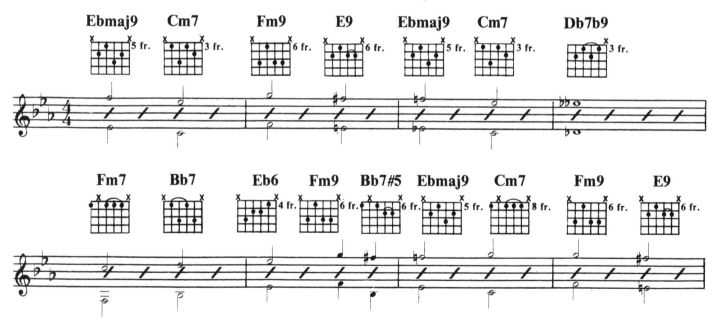

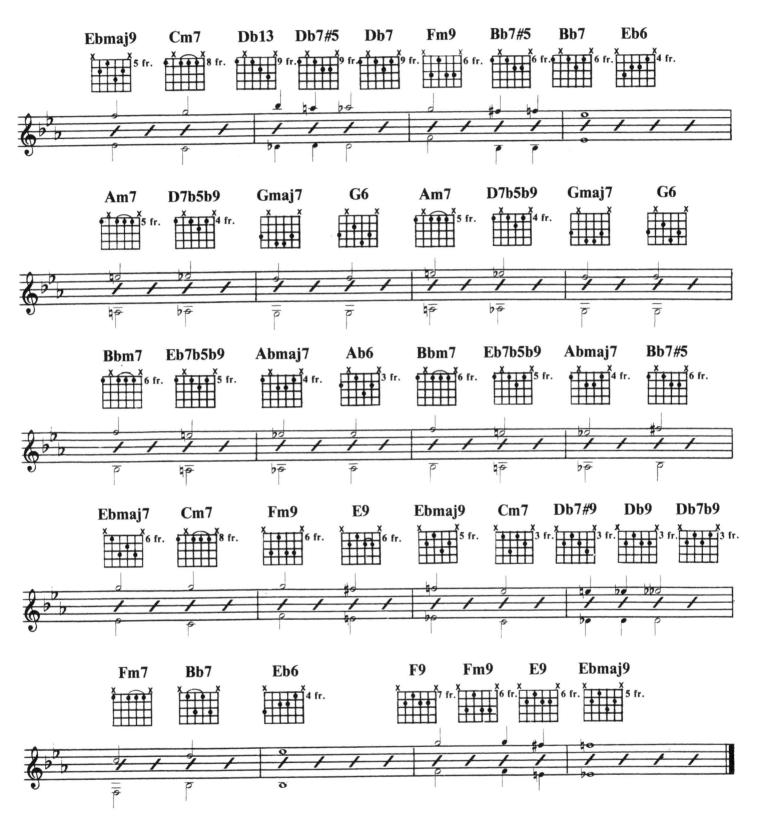

When using chord embellishments be sure that there is no conflict with the melody. For example, if you are accompanying a singer or an instrumentalist who is holding a melody note D, do not play a G7b5 or G7#5 since the Db (b5) or the D# (#5) will clash with the natural D. You can play the altered chord if you do not stay on it but pass through it to a more consonant chord. If you are accompanying an instrumentalist who is improvising then you can play as many chord embellishments as you wish since it will provide a colorful background for his improvisations.

Chord Substitutions

A chord substitute is a chord used to *replace* another chord. The substitute chord will have a new root or letter name.

Rules for Chord Substitution

One chord can be used in place of another when both the substitute chord and the original chord have two or more common tones.

To illustrate this, look at the the harmonized scale once again.

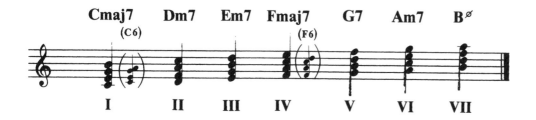

Notice that by extending the Cmaj7 chord to a Cmaj9 we have four tones in common with the Em7 chord.

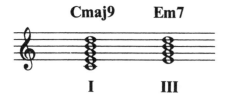

Below are the chord forms showing the Cmaj9 with the fifth in the bass and the Em7 with the third in the bass. The fingering is exactly the same.

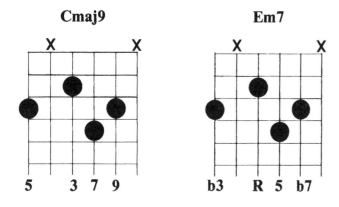

The notes contained in the Cmaj9 chord are C, E, G, B, and D. The notes in the Em7 chord are E, G, B, and D. Because of the common tones between the two chords we can conclude that the Em7 chord is a substitute for the Cmaj9 chord. Or, we can say that the III chord is a substitute for the I chord.

By the same process we can look at the C6 chord (C, E, G, and A) and the Am7 chord (A, C, E, and G) and conclude that the VI chord is also a substitute for the I chord. The two chord forms are the same.

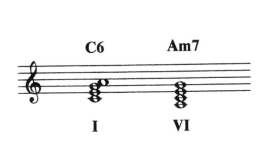

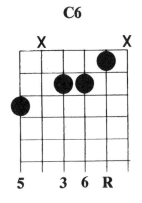

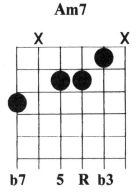

Table of Substitute Chords for the I Chord

I chord	*III chord*	*VI chord*
C	Em7	Am7
F	Am7	Dm7
Bb	Dm7	Gm7
Eb	Gm7	Cm7
Ab	Cm7	Fm7
Db	Fm7	Bbm7
Gb	Bbm7	Ebm7
B	D#m7	G#m7
E	G#m7	C#m7
A	C#m7	F#m7
D	F#m7	Bm7
G	Bm7	Em7

The I chords listed above do not indicate whether they are major seventh or major sixth since in most cases both chords are interchangeable. However, if a sixth chord is indicated it is usually best to use the VI as the substitute. Once again your ear is the final judge. Listen to how the melody note determines which is the best chord to use for the substitution.

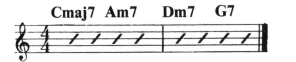

Another kind of chord substitution is to replace one chord with another of the *same letter name* but a different quality.

In the progressions shown above, in substituting the Em7 for the Cmaj7 (III for I) it would be best to substitute an A7 for the Am7. By using chord substitution, what started out as a I-VI progression in the first measure (Cmaj7-Am7) is now a II-V progression (Em7-A7).

Any dominant seventh chord can be replaced by another dominant seventh built on the *flatted fifth* of the original chord. For example, you can substitute an Ab7 for a D7. Ab being the flatted fifth of the D7. The two most important notes of any chord are the third and the seventh and these two notes are common to both chords.

Original chord D7 = D, F#, A and C
b5 substitute Ab7 = Ab, C, Eb and Gb

Note that the F# (third) and the C (seventh) of the D7 become the seventh and the third of the Ab7 chord. (F# is the enharmonic equivalent of Gb).

In the arrangement of the standard popular tune on page 56 you will find, in the thirteenth measure, the chord symbol D7b5b9. The chord diagram illustrates what you have learned is an Ab7 chord. The Ab7 is the flatted fifth substitute of the D7b5b9 chord. The substitute chord is actually another form of the *original* dominant chord embellished with a b5 and a b9.

Original chord D7b5b9 = D, F#, Ab, C and Eb
b5 substitute Ab7 = Ab, C, Eb, and Gb

The root of the Ab7 is the flatted fifth of the D7, the third of the Ab7 is the seventh of the D7, the fifth of the Ab7 is the flatted ninth of the D7, and the seventh of the Ab7 is the third of the D7.

We can conclude that the flatted fifth substitute is actually an embellished version of the original dominant seventh chord. Ab7 is actually a D7b5b9 without the root.

Table of Flatted Fifth Substitutes for the V7 Chord

C7	*Gb7*
F7	*B7*
Bb7	*E7*
Eb7	*A7*
Ab7	*D7*
Db7	*G7*
F#7	*C7*
B7	*F7*
E7	*Bb7*
A7	*Eb7*
D7	*Ab7*
G7	*Db7*

The following progression illustrates the III for I substitution, the change of chord quality substitution, and the flatted fifth substitution.

	Gmaj7	Em7		Am7	D7		Gmaj7				
Original progression	/ /	/ /	|	/ /	/ /	|	/ /	/ /	|	/ /	/ / ||

	Bm7	E7		Am7	Ab7		Gmaj7				
Substitute progression	/ /	/ /	|	/ /	/ /	|	/ /	/ /	|	/ /	/ / ||
	III for I	**Change of quality**			**b5**						

In the first measure of the substitute progression, since we've changed the quality of the Em7 to E7 we can now use the flatted fifth substitution and create a progression which gives us a descending chromatic bass line.

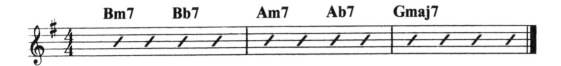

Below is another example of the use of the flatted fifth substitution. The substitute chord is being used along with the original chord in the same measure. Note also that both the original chord and the substitute chord are embellished.

Original progression:

Substitute progression:

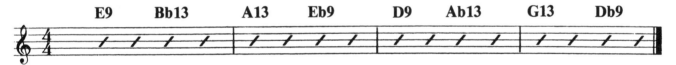

Looking back once again to page 56, the E9 chord in the second, eighth, twenty-second, and twenty-seventh measures is an extended or embellished chord and is the flatted fifth substitute for the Bb7 which would normally be played between the Fm7 and the Eb chord (II–V–I). By using the flatted fifth substitute we created a descending, chromatic bass line (Fm9–E9–Ebmaj9).

Delaying Resolution

There is a natural tendency for the dominant seventh (V) chord to want to move to the tonic (I) chord. This is due to the fact that in the dominant seventh are two notes which have a very strong pull toward the tonic chord. The third of the dominant seventh has a strong pull toward the root of the tonic chord and the seventh of the dominant seventh has a pull toward the third of the tonic chord. In the G7 for example, the B pulls toward the C of the C chord and the F of the G7 pulls toward the E of the C chord. The third and seventh of the dominant seventh are known as the *tritone*, and it is the tension created by this tritone that wants to be resolved by going to the tonic chord.

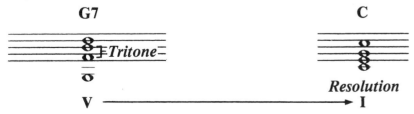

One of the most effective ways of creating a sense of continuity and flow in music is to use devices which delay resolution to the tonic chord. One is to use a series of dominant seventh chords as shown on page 61 in the original progression, E7-A7-D7-G7. To heighten the feeling of the tension even further, there is a general rule in jazz that *all dominant seventh (V) chords are preceded by a minor seventh (II) chord.* In order to know the II chord, you must figure out which key each V7 chord is in. In our original progression the E7 is the V of the key of A, so the II chord is Bm7. The A7 is the V of the key of D so the II chord is Em7. The D7 is the V chord in the key of G so the II chord is Am7 and the G7 is the V in the key of C so the II chord is Dm7. Below we see the original progression which now includes the IIm7 chords:

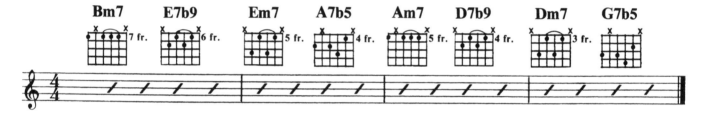

Here is a suggested fingering for the above progression. Note the slight alteration in the dominant seventh chords which creates an interesting line.

The Tritone

The tritone which we briefly discussed on page 61 is an interval of three whole tones or whole steps. It is this tritone which creates the forward motion or the sense of wanting to resolve to the I chord. It is also the reason for the flatted fifth substitution chord being able to take the place of the V chord. *The flatted fifth chord contains the same tritone as the dominant seventh chord which it replaces.* For example, the notes in the G7 chord are G, B, D and F. The tritone is B to F. The notes in the flatted fifth substitute chord Db7 are Db, F, Ab and Cb. The tritone is F to Cb (B). The two notes of the tritone are in both chords; only the order is reversed. The third and seventh of the G7 now become the seventh and third of the Db7.

The Diminished Seventh Chord

The diminished seventh chord is a very useful and interesting chord. Let's see where it comes from. Below is a listing of the notes contained in four dominant seventh flatted ninth chords. By omitting the root of these chords we see that the remaining notes form a diminished seventh chord. The four diminished seventh chords contain exactly the same notes (allowing for enharmonic equivalents), so we can conclude that all four chords, C, D#, F# and A diminished seventh (°7) are the same chord.

Dominant seventh flatted ninth chords
Ab7b9 = Ab–C–Eb–Gb–Bbb (A)
B7b9 = B–D#–F#–A–C
D7b9 = D–F#–A–C–Eb ·
F7b9 = F–A–C–Eb–Gb

Diminished seventh chords
C°7 = C–Eb–Gb–Bbb (A)
D#°7 = D#–F#–A–C
F#°7 = F#–A–C–Eb
A°7 = A–C–Eb–Gb

Below are four more dominant seventh flatted ninth chords and the diminished seventh chords formed from each:

Dominant seventh flatted ninth chords
A7b9 = A–C#–E–G–Bb
C7b9 = C–E–G–Bb–Db
Eb7b9 = Eb–G–Bb–Db–Fb
Gb7b9 = Gb–Bb–Db–Fb–Abb (G)

Diminished seventh chords
C#°7 = C#–E–G–Bb
E°7 = E–G–Bb–Db
G°7 = G–Bb–Db–Fb–Abb (G)
Bb°7 = Bb–Db–Fb–Abb (G)

We can conclude from the above that C#, E, G and Bb diminished seventh are all the same chord.

Below are the last four dominant seventh flatted ninth chords and the diminished seventh chords formed from each:

Dominant seventh flatted ninth chords
Bb7b9 = Bb–D–F–Ab–Cb
Db7b9 = Db–F–Ab–Cb–Ebb (D)
E7b9 = E–G#–B–D–F
G7b9 = G–B–D–F–Ab

Diminished seventh chords
D°7 = D–F–Ab–Cb
F°7 = F–Ab–Cb–Ebb (D)
G#°7 = G#–B–D–F
B°7 = B–D–F–Ab

We can conclude from the above that D, F, G# and B diminished seventh chords are the same chord.

To summarize the material above we can say that there are basically three different diminished seventh chords with each having four possible names and four possible roots plus their enharmonic equivalents. (*See* Appendix.)

The two fingerings most often used for the diminished seventh chords are shown below. One is off the sixth string and one is off the fifth string. Play both forms up the fingerboard and learn all the possible names for each chord at each fret.

G°7–Bb°7–Db°7–E°7

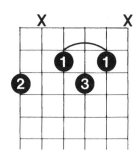

C°7–Eb°7–Gb°7–A°7

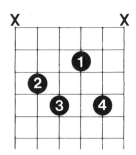

The most common use of a diminished seventh chord is as a passing chord between two chords, creating a chromatic moving bass line.

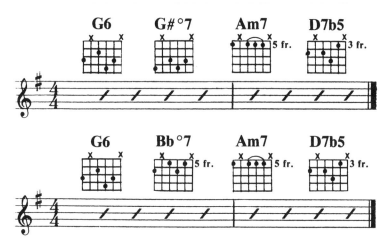

Another example of the use of diminished seventh chords to create a chromatic bass line.

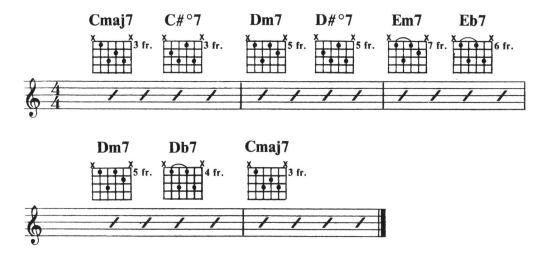

Diminished Seventh Chord Substitutions

The root of the diminished seventh chord is the third of a dominant seventh flatted ninth chord, therefore, we can reverse that rule and form a dominant seventh chord from a diminished seventh chord. For example, looking back to page 63 we see that by omitting the root of the Ab7b9 chord we are left with a C°7 chord. Now to reverse that, when we see a C°7 chord we may substitute the Ab7 chord (or Ab7b9). To carry this one step further, a dominant seventh chord may be preceded by a IIm7 chord so we can place the Ebm7 in front of the Ab7. We now have two chords in place of one. The substitution for the C°7 chord is Ebm7–Ab7.

The following table lists the II–V substitution for each diminished seventh chord.

Diminished chord	II	V
		substitution
C°7	Ebm7	Ab7
Eb°7	F#m7	B7
Gb°7 or F#°7	Am7	D7
A°7	Cm7	F7
C#°7	Em7	A7
E°7	Gm7	C7
G°7	Bbm7	Eb7
Bb°7	C#m7	F#m7 (Dbm7 Gb7)
D°7	Fm7	Bb7
F°7	Abm7	Db7
Ab°7	Bm7	E7
B°7	Dm7	G7

Remember: Since each diminished seventh chord has four possible names, then each chord has four possible II–V substitutions. For example, a C°7 may be replaced by either Ebm7–Ab7, F#m7–B7, Am7–D7, or Cm7–F7. Let your ear be the judge as to which II–V substitute works best. There must be no conflict with the melody.

Original progression

Substitute progression

The diminished seventh chord having four possible roots or letter names means that we can change the root of a diminished seventh chord in order to create a moving line in the bass. Below is a progression in which the diminished seventh chord has the same root as the I chord. By substituting the III chord for the I (Bm7 for Gmaj7), then changing the G°7 chord to a Bb°7 we have created a descending chromatic bass line. To further continue the downward direction of the line we can use the flatted fifth substitute for the D7 in the fourth measure.

Original progression

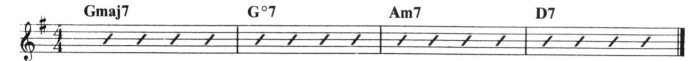

Substitute progression

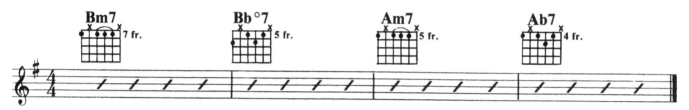

Because of the ease with which diminished seventh chords may be played up and down the fingerboard they are often used to provide a smooth, symmetrical movement into a I chord. For example, below, a series of diminished seventh chords substitutes for a II-V progression resolving into a I chord.

Original progression

Substitute progression

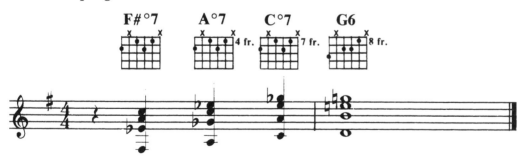

A variation on the use of the diminished seventh chords is to create a chord–scale line motion resolving to the I chord. This is done by using the fourth finger to play a single note connecting one diminished seventh chord form to the next. The notes in the top line of the following example form a *diminished scale.* *

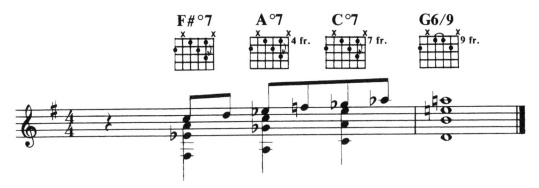

* A diminished scale is formed by adding a note one whole step above each chord tone. For example, a C diminished seventh chord consists of C–Eb–Gb–A. Adding a note one whole step above each chord tone gives us C–D–Eb–F–Gb–Ab–A–B, the C diminished scale.

The following illustrates a descending variation on the above progression. Notice that the final G6 chord contains only three notes.

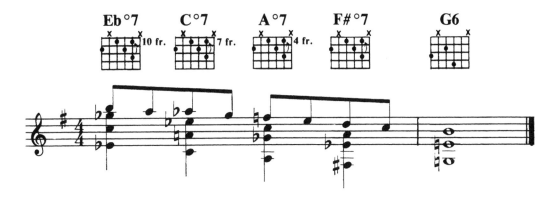

The diminished seventh chord may actually be moved in any direction up or down the fingerboard and ultimately will lead into the I chord. The important thing is to be sure that the chord which precedes the I chord is the correct chord. For example, in the following two measure exercise, the I chord is the G6. In the measure before the G6, start on a C°7 and then play series of diminished seventh chords ending with another C°7 which leads well into the G6.

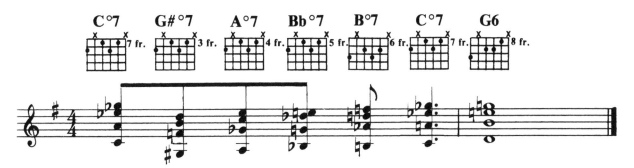

Parallel Chromatic Chord Movement

Parallel chromatic chord movement refers to all the notes of a chord moving chromatically either up or down to another chord. This may resolve directly into a tonic (I) chord or into the dominant chord (V) which then resolves to the tonic (I) chord. In the example just given the chromatic movement began with the G# diminished seventh chord and moved chromatically upward till reaching the C diminished seventh. The C diminished seventh is simply a D7b9 chord which is the V of the G6. Below is an example of parallel chromatic movement.

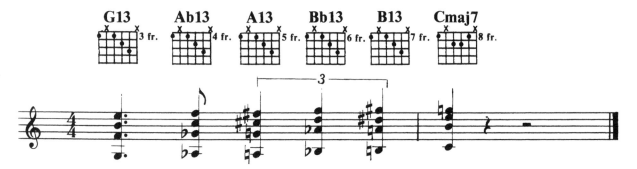

All chords may be approached by another chord which is either a half step above or below. G7, for instance, may be approached by Ab7 (above) or F#7 (below).

Original progression

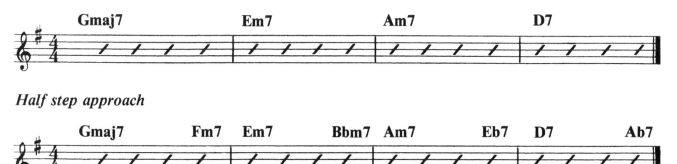

Half step approach

Dominant Sevenths with Suspended Fourths

A suspension in jazz harmony is usually created by raising the third of the dominant seventh chord. This suspended tone is foreign to the basic harmony and sets up a feeling of tension which is resolved as the raised third is followed by the natural third. The symbol for the suspended chord is sus 4. The four indicates the third of the chord is replaced by the fourth.

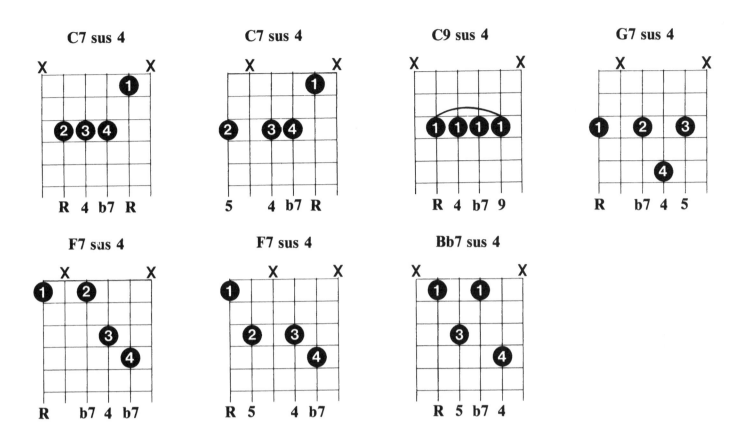

C7 sus 4   R 4 b7 R

C7 sus 4   5 4 b7 R

C9 sus 4   R 4 b7 9

G7 sus 4   R b7 4 5

F7 sus 4   R b7 4 b7

F7 sus 4   R 5 4 b7

Bb7 sus 4   R 5 b7 4

The following examples illustrate the use of suspended chords.

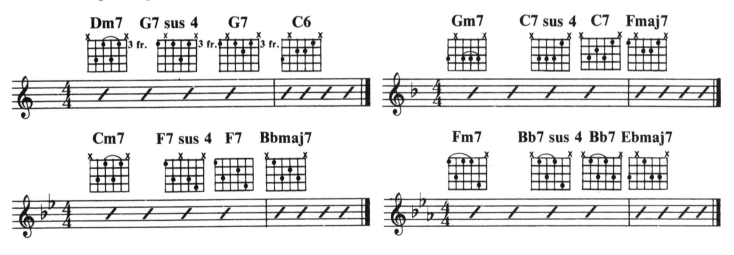

Three Part Open Voiced Chords

A chord voicing popularized by Freddie Green, guitarist with the Count Basie band, and later used by many of the top rhythm guitarists such as Bucky Pizzarelli and Barry Galbraith, is the three note open voiced chord voicing shown below. Note that the chords use only the sixth, fourth, and third strings. The fifth string is muted. The chord formations are basically the same as the forms you have already learned but without the second string.

Root on sixth string:

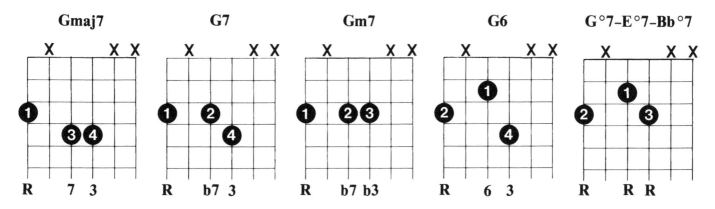

Third on sixth string:

These forms are limited in the three part open voicing since the various kinds of sevenths are on the second string and it is the second string that is omitted.

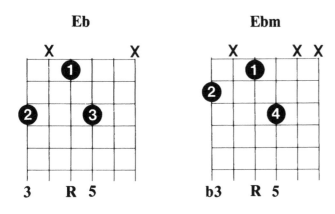

Fifth on sixth string:

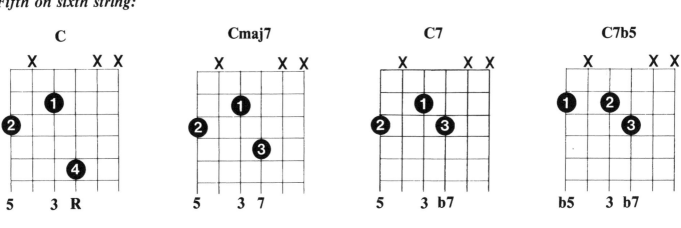

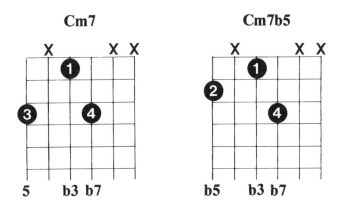

When playing these three note chords it is important to understand that when you see chord symbols such as C7b9#11 or C13#9, etc. all that is really required is that you play a C7 chord. All the upper parts such as ninths, elevenths and thirteenths are probably being played by other instruments in the band. The job of the guitarist is simply to keep the momentum of the rhythm going. Also it is not necessary to play the root or the fifth of a chord since the bass player will usually be playing those notes.

Progressions with Three Note Chords

The following progressions illustrate the use of the three note open voiced chords. Play these progressions in other keys until you get the feel of them.

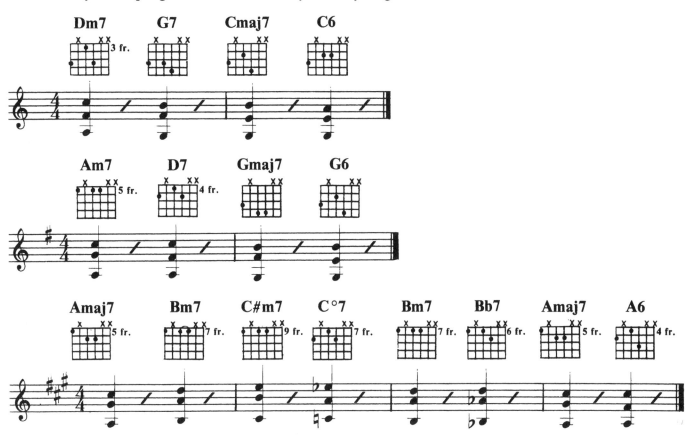

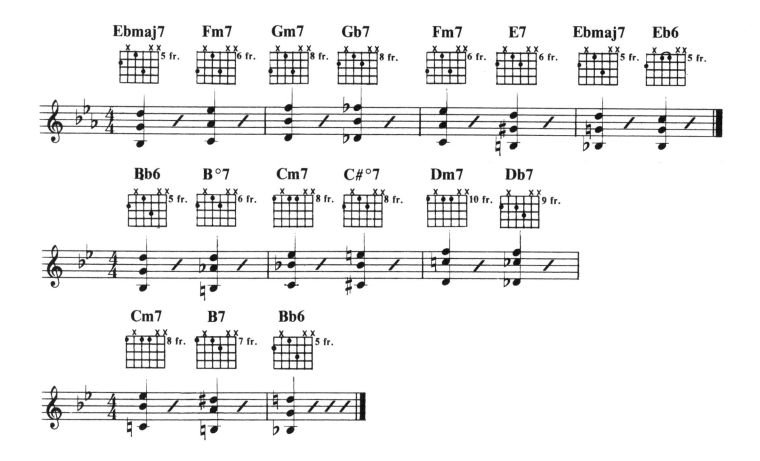

Three Note Chords with Their Root on the Fifth String

Three note open voiced chords may also be played with the root on the fifth string. These chords have exactly the same voicing as the three note chords whose root is on the sixth string.

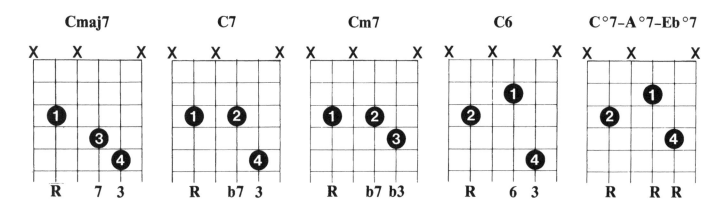

The following chord forms also have their root on the fifth string, however, their voicings are different.

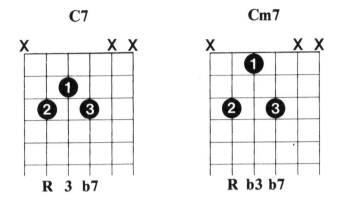

Below we see how the same progression may be played in two different areas of the fingerboard using the *same voicing*.

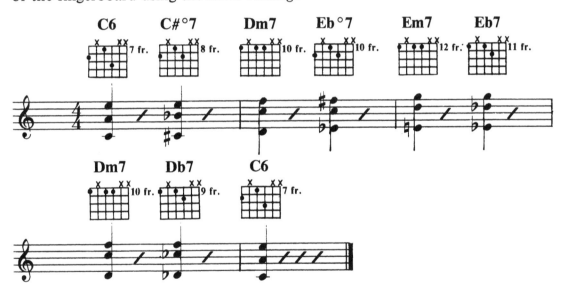

Here is the same progression, using the same voicing, with the root on the fifth string. You are now playing closer to the neck of the fingerboard, where the sound is a little fuller.

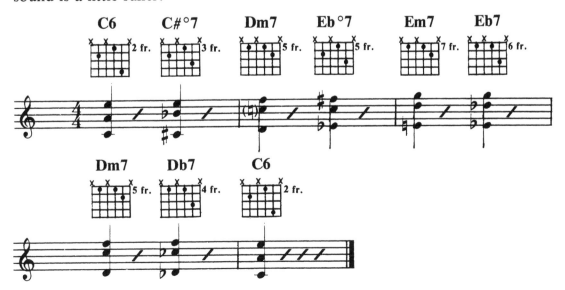

Combining Chords Having Their Root on the Fifth and Sixth Strings

The following studies illustrate how you can play some commonly used progressions and keep the roots in the bass without jumping all over the fingerboard.

Blues with Three Note Chords

Here is an example of how the blues might be played using only three note open voiced chords. These chords are used by many of the leading rhythm guitar players such as Freddie Green of the Count Basie band.

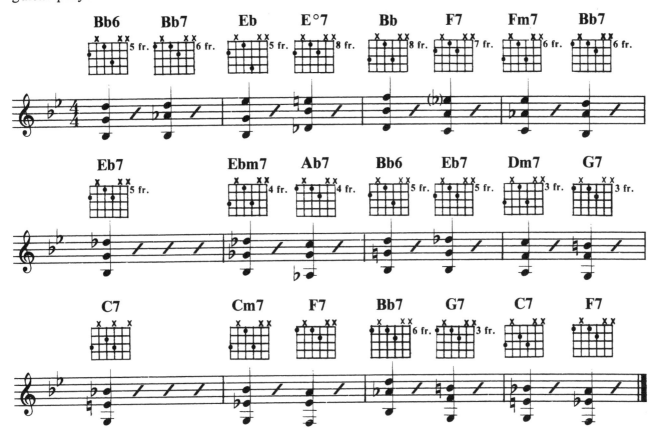

All the above chord forms are based off the sixth string. The same kind of voicings may be used by combining chords such as these with chords based off the fifth string. Try experimenting with such voicings.

The Half Step Approach Chords

On page 68 we learned that any chord may be preceded by another chord (usually some form of dominant seventh), whose root is a *half step above or below the chord you're going to.* For example, here is the familiar I–VI–II–V progression:

Note that the VI chord is played as a dominant seventh (G7) rather than the normal minor seventh (Gm7).

Here is the same progression with the added chords one half step above the given chord. The descending movement from the half step approach chord to the original chord may be considered descending parallel movement:

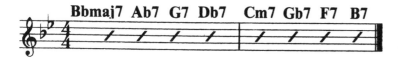

Here are some of the ways this may be played on the fingerboard:

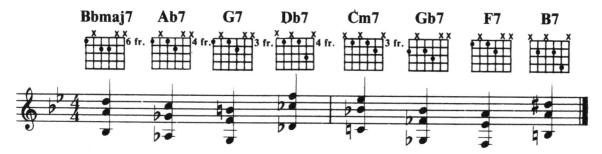

Here is the same progression with the half step approach chord below the original chord. The ascending movement from the approach chord to the original chord may be considered ascending parallel movement:

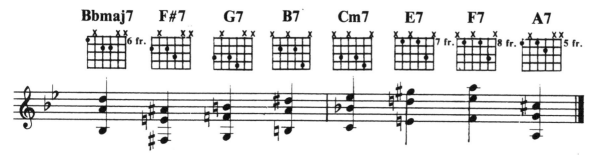

Below are more ways to play the basic I–VI–II–V progression with the added approach chords. Some of the chords are played with the fifth in the bass. The approach chord on the fourth beat in the first measure is the same quality as the chord it is going to. This makes for better voice leading.

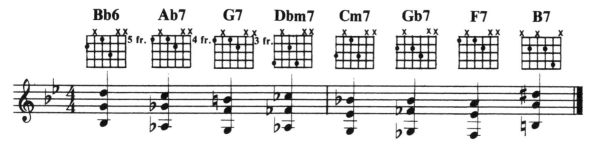

Another way to play the same progression:

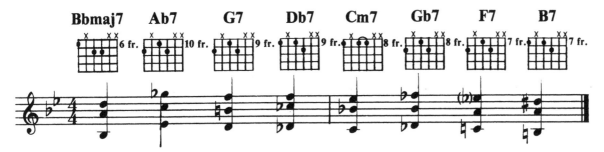

All these progressions may also be played with the fuller four string chord forms. The advantage to the three note forms is that they are easier to move around, especially when playing a chord on every beat. Also, using these three note chords gives more uniformity in voicings.

The Harmonized Scale

If you look back to page 41 you will see reference made to the harmonized scale. The harmonized scale is the harmonizing of each note in any particular scale. For a review let's look at the F major harmonized scale.

F major harmonized scale

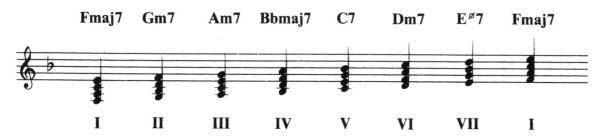

Let's see how the F major harmonized scale may be played. We will use the four note chord form.

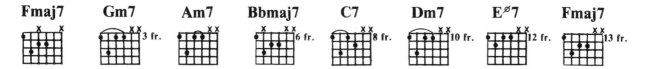

Note that the chord forms shown above use the sixth, fifth, and fourth strings, the bottom set of four strings. To avoid having to play the scale all the way up to the thirteenth fret and to keep the sound quality of the chords the same (the sound thins out higher up on the board), you can switch to the middle set of four strings and play the upper part of the scale on those strings. The voicing of the chords is exactly the same.

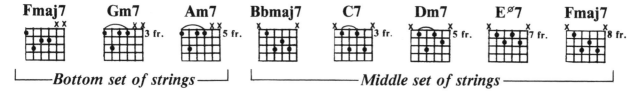

Here we see the G major harmonized scale played on the two sets of strings.

G major harmonized scale

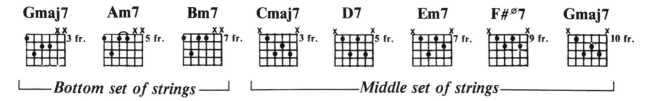

Note that in the above harmonized scale I chose to switch to the middle set of strings on the Cmaj7 chord. I could have switched at the Bm7 if I wanted to. Make the switch wherever you find it most convenient.

Harmonized Scale with Three Note Chords

The harmonized scales can also be played with the three note open voiced chords and are quite often used that way.

F major harmonized scale

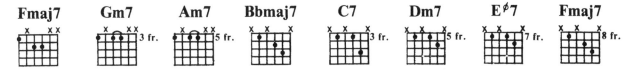

The E$^\phi$7 (Em7b5) chord diagram doesn't show the flatted fifth, because in the three note chords the fifth is omitted.

G major harmonized scale

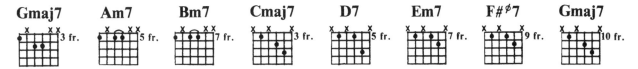

Practice playing *all* the harmonized scales using both the four note and the three note chord forms.

Harmonized Scales with Passing Chords

There are a number of ways in which passing chords can be used to connect the chords of the harmonized scale. It will be shown soon that this is a very commonly used device to enrich a rather bland progression.

1. Diminished seventh passing chords

The following harmonized scale uses the diminished seventh chord to connect each of the chords in the scale. Notice that although four note chords are shown, you should practice the same study using three note chords.

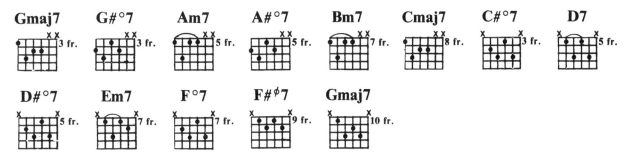

2. Secondary dominant seventh chords

The following harmonized scale uses a dominant seventh chord to lead into each of the diatonic chords. Each diatonic chord acts as a temporary I chord and the dominant seventh acts as a V chord going to the I. Notice that the dominant seventh chords have the fifth in the bass.

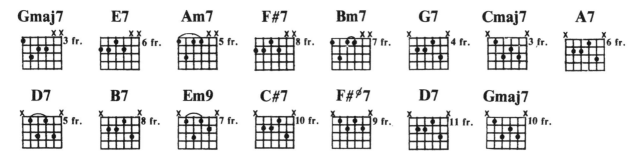

The preceding study can also be played using the three note open voiced chords. Some of the fingerings are illustrated below.

Root on sixth string   *Fifth on sixth string*   *Fifth on fifth string*

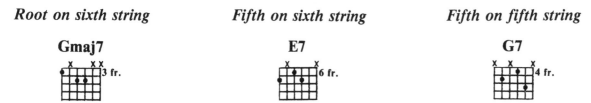

3. Half step chromatic approach

This last variation of the harmonized scale uses the half step chromatic approach. Each diatonic chord is approached by a chord of the *same quality*, a half step below.

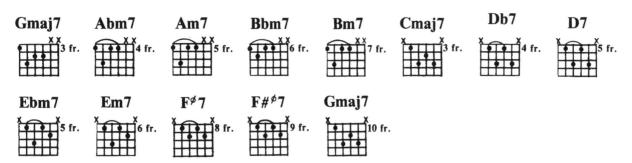

Also practice the above study using the three note open voiced chords.

With the limited amount of chord forms that we've studied so far it's obvious that you can't play all of the harmonized scales within the practical range of the guitar fingerboard. If you play the inverted forms of the chords you can increase the scales available. Below is the C major harmonized scale with the fifth in the bass.

| Cmaj7 | Dm7 | Em7 | Fmaj7 | G7 | Am7 | B⌀7 | Cmaj7 |

Playing harmonized scales all over the fingerboard is one of the best ways of developing chord facility.

Connecting Chords—Harmonized Bass Lines

In the section on Connecting Chords with Bass Runs (see page 18), we learned how it is possible to connect one chord to another by using a series of single notes called a bass run. At that point we were working with simple open string chords. However, this same device may also be used with jazz chords. We will take this device a step further, add chords to these bass runs and call them harmonized bass lines.

Here is progression made up of four chords. Each chord is connected to the one which follows by a single note bass run.

Here is the same progression with each of the single notes harmonized creating a harmonized bass line.

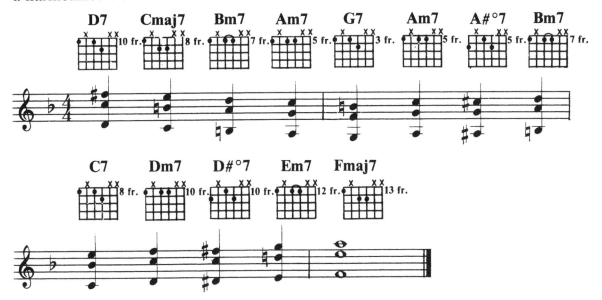

Analysis of Bass Line

Below is an analysis of the harmonized bass line you have just played. This should help you to better understand just what is involved so that you may apply the principles to your own playing.

Measure one. The D7 is thought of as the V chord to the G7 chord in the second measure. Thinking of the G7 as a temporary I, all we did was to descend the harmonized scale till reaching the G7.

Measure two. Think of the G7 as the V of the C7 in the third measure. The C7 is a temporary I, so move up the harmonized scale to the C7 chord. The A# diminished seventh chord is used to connect the Am7 to the Bm7 and to create a delay in order not to reach the C7 a beat too soon.

Measure three. Think of the C7 as the V of the F chord in the fourth measure and move up the harmonized scale, using the D# diminished seventh chord to connect the Dm7 to the Em7 and also to delay reaching the F major seventh chord too soon.

Another way to create a harmonized bass line is to alternate between a V chord and the II chord plus diminished seventh passing chords and half step approach chords.

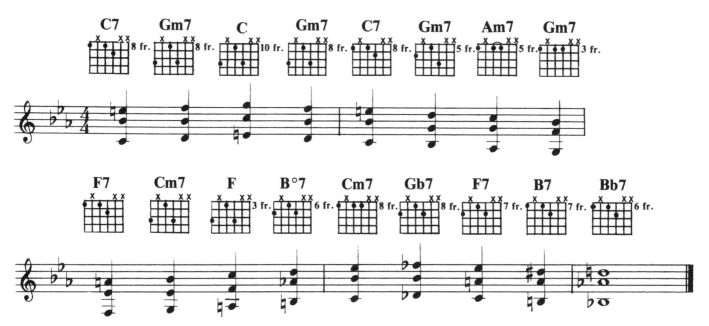

Here is an analysis of the harmonized bass line shown above.

Measure one. Note how the C7 chord alternates with its II chord, the Gm7. The Gm7 is played with the fifth in the bass.

Measure two. Here again the first beat is the V chord followed by its II chord. The Am7 is a passing chord between the Gm7 chords. It connects the Gm7, third in the bass to the Gm7, root in the bass.

Measure three. The F7 alternates with the Cm7, its II chord. The B diminished seventh chord is a passing chord moving to the Cm7 in the next measure.

Measure four. The Gb7 is a half step approach chord to the F7. The B7 is a half step approach chord to the Bb7.

In this method of harmonizing the bass line, the inner voices move less than when using the harmonized scale movement; it's more important that the outside voices move. The outside voices create the forward motion so desired in this type of playing.

Below is an example of how a harmonized bass line may be used to fill in a measure where there is only one chord for the full measure.

The Bm7 is the III chord substituting for the G chord. So in effect it's like being back on the Gmaj7.

Below is an example of how a harmonized bass line can be used to fill in two measures of the same chord. In this example it is a Cmaj7 chord.

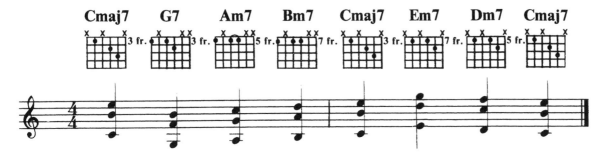

All of the above chords are contained within the original C major harmonized scale structure and so the feeling of the key of C major is still very strong. It is not necessary to always have chromatic or diatonic movement in the line. It is possible to make a jump such as the Cmaj7 to the G7 in the first measure or the Cmaj7 to the Em7 in the second measure.

Blues Progression and Harmonized Bass Line

The blues progression offers the best possibilities for the use of harmonized bass lines because of the openness of the structure. In other words, there are few chords in the blues, so in order to create an interesting accompaniment, and to give a feeling of forward motion, the harmonized bass line is an advantageous device.

Below are two choruses of blues. The first chorus is a rather simple
harmonized bass line.

In this next chorus of the blues, note that in the second measure we use the three note open voiced chords based on the fifth string. If you prefer to play the chords up on the higher frets of the guitar you may do so.

Chords on the Top Four Strings

The chords played on the top four strings are very useful for two reasons. They are used for a certain style of accompaniment known as "comping;" this is where the guitarist doesn't play a steady four beats to the measure but instead plays chords in a very rhythmic manner, feeding chords to the soloist and pushing him along at the same time. The second reason is that they are used for "chord melody" playing, that is, playing chords and melody at the same time.

Learning the chords on the top four strings is not as much of a problem as you might think, because most of them are based on chord forms you already know. For example, the top string (first string) is the E string and the sixth string is also an E string (two octaves lower), therefore any chord you already know which has either its root, third, fifth or seventh on the sixth string can have that note which is on the sixth string moved up to the first string. See below:

Gmaj7 (Root on sixth string)

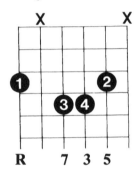

R 7 3 5

Gmaj7 (Root on first string)

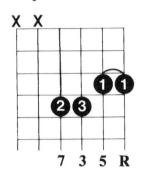

7 3 5 R

The root is taken from the sixth string and placed on the first string. This can be done with all the chords you already know.

Chords with Their Root on the First String

G

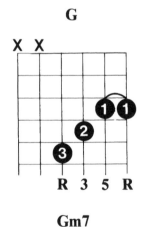

R 3 5 R

Gmaj7

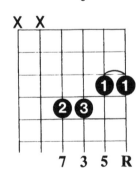

7 3 5 R

G7

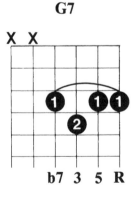

b7 3 5 R

G6

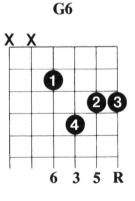

6 3 5 R

Gm7

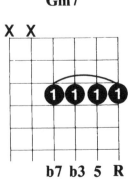

b7 b3 5 R

Gm7b5

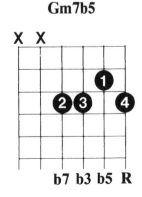

b7 b3 b5 R

Gm6

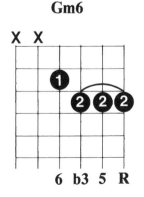

6 b3 5 R

G7#5

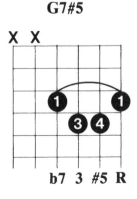

b7 3 #5 R

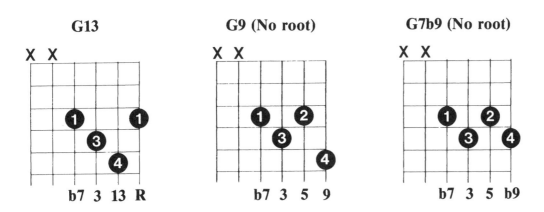

Play all of the above chord forms up the fingerboard and be sure you know the relative position of each note on each string within the chord. For example, you should know that the fifth of the chord is on the second string, the third of the chord is on the third string, etc.

Chords with Their Third on the First String

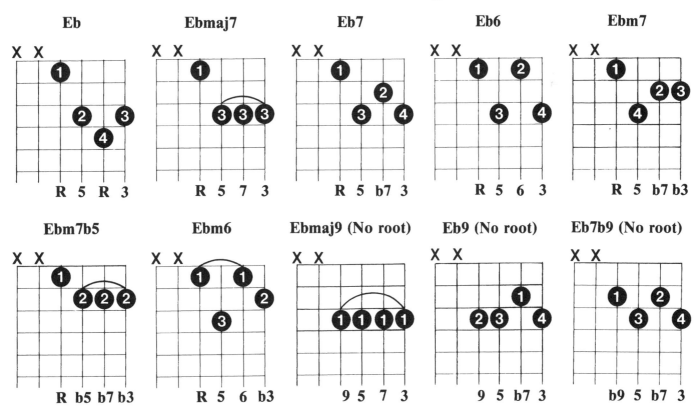

These chords with the third on the first string also have the root in the bass (fourth string). They can be used to expand the harmonized scale possibilities.

Chords with Their Fifth on the First String

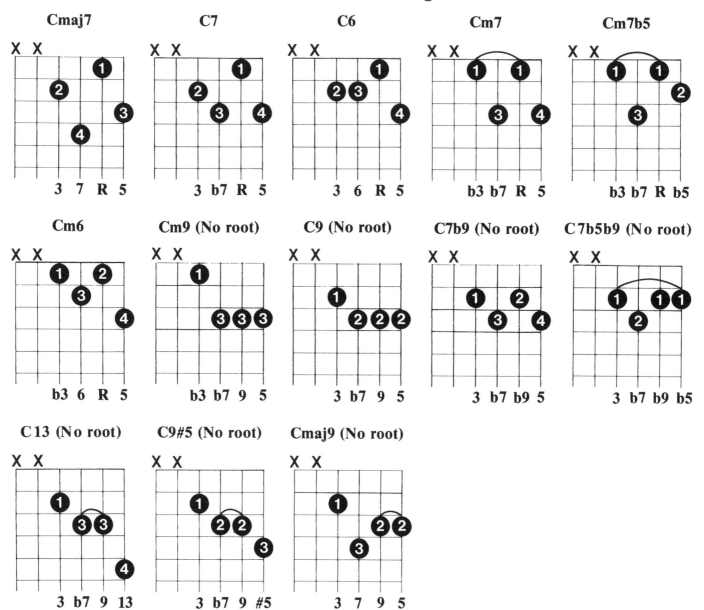

Cmaj7 — 3 7 R 5
C7 — 3 b7 R 5
C6 — 3 6 R 5
Cm7 — b3 b7 R 5
Cm7b5 — b3 b7 R b5

Cm6 — b3 6 R 5
Cm9 (No root) — b3 b7 9 5
C9 (No root) — 3 b7 9 5
C7b9 (No root) — 3 b7 b9 5
C7b5b9 (No root) — 3 b7 b9 b5

C13 (No root) — 3 b7 9 13
C9#5 (No root) — 3 b7 9 #5
Cmaj9 (No root) — 3 7 9 5

Chords with Their Seventh on the First String

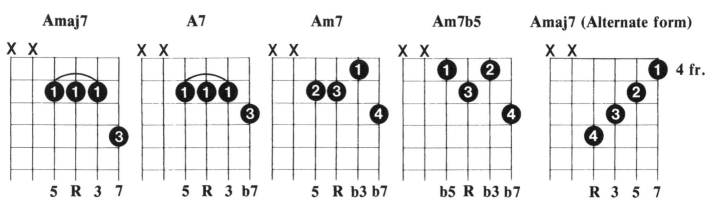

Amaj7 — 5 R 3 7
A7 — 5 R 3 b7
Am7 — 5 R b3 b7
Am7b5 — b5 R b3 b7
Amaj7 (Alternate form) — R 3 5 7 — 4 fr.

Chords with Their Ninth on the First String

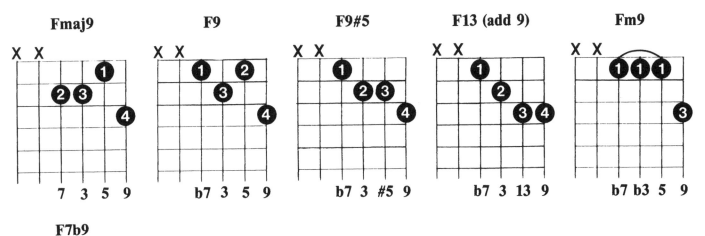

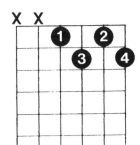

Note that in all the ninth chords there is no root. Moving the root two frets up creates the ninth chord.

It is important that all of the chords in this section be played all over the fingerboard to attain smoothness in playing at any fret.

Probably the best exercise at this point would be to start with the Fmaj7 at the first fret and play all the inversions; root on the first string, third on the first string, fifth on the first string, seventh on the first string and ninth on the first string. Do the same with all the different chord qualities.

For those chords that cannot be played on the higher frets due to the shortness of the fingerboard or the narrowness of the frets, drop down to the lower part of the fingerboard. Some chords may have to be played starting with the third or the fifth on the first string in order to make full use of the fingerboard. In other words all the C chords may be started with the fifth on the first string, then move up to the seventh, the root and the ninth.

Harmonized Scales Extended to the Top Four Strings

Those chords with the third on the first string have their root on the fourth string or in the bass. With that in mind we can play some more harmonized scales extending them into the top strings. Below is the Bb scale starting with the root on the fifth string. Starting with the IV chord, the Ebmaj7, we can move up to the root on the fourth string.

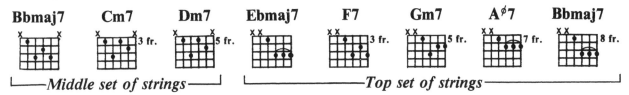

Another way of playing the harmonized scale is to play all the chords with the fifth in the bass. Below is the C harmonized scale played on the three sets of strings; the bottom set of four, the middle set of four and the top set of four.

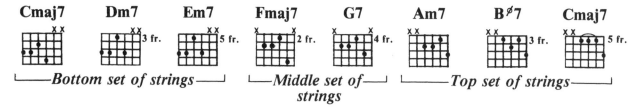

Cmaj7   Dm7   Em7   Fmaj7   G7   Am7   B∅7   Cmaj7

└──*Bottom set of strings*──┘ └──*Middle set of*──┘ └──*Top set of strings*──┘
                                      strings

Play as many harmonized scales as you can across all three sets of four strings. Play them with the root in the bass and with the fifth in the bass. Also play scales with passing chords and secondary dominant sevenths as shown on pages 79 and 80.

Additional Chords

The following chord forms are very useful and should be added to your repertoire of chord forms.

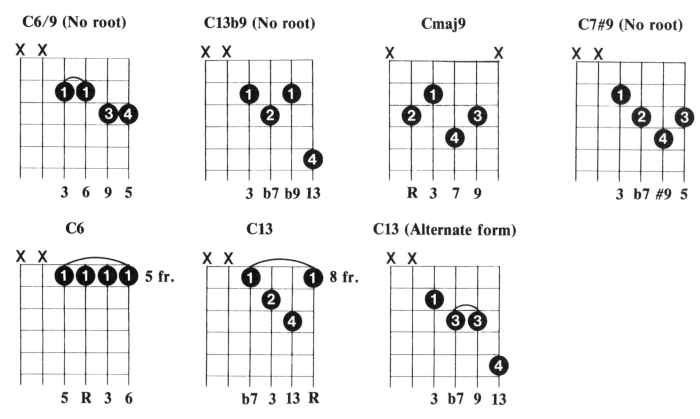

C6/9 (No root)   C13b9 (No root)   Cmaj9   C7#9 (No root)

3 6 9 5   3 b7 b9 13   R 3 7 9   3 b7 #9 5

C6   C13   C13 (Alternate form)

5 R 3 6   b7 3 13 R   3 b7 9 13

Combining Chords on Middle and Top Strings

Let's work on the middle and top four string chords. Below are a series of chord studies based on the ever popular II–V–I chord progression in a number of different keys. Play them over and over until they're played with no hesitation. All the chords have their root in the bass.

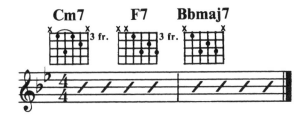

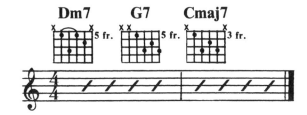

The preceding study should be played up the fingerboard as far as you can go.
Do the same with the following series of chords.

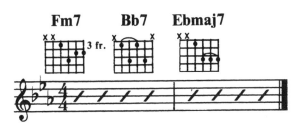

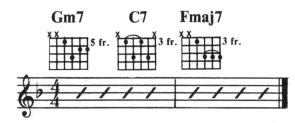

The following series of chords have the fifth in the bass to the third in the bass to the root in the bass. Again, play up the fingerboard.

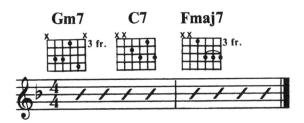

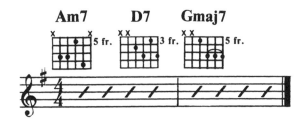

Comping

The responsibility of a rhythm guitarist is to define the chord changes on which an improvisor bases a solo. One type of rhythm guitar playing is to simply play chords on each beat of the measure. However, in recent years the role of the guitar player has been expanded. The modern guitarist must be knowledgeable in three areas.

1. A thorough knowledge of chord voicings is necessary in order to control not only the bass line but also the direction and melodic flow of the top voice of each chord.
2. Complete control over a great variety of rhythm patterns beyond just playing a chord on every beat.
3. How to create rhythm patterns so that they relate to the melody of a given tune or to an improvised solo.

This new expanded role of the guitar player is called "comping" and we will explore that style of accompaniment now.

Chord Voicings with Melodic Top Line

When comping it is generally best to move from chord to chord in as smooth a manner as possible. Do not jump from one area of the fingerboard to another. Most good rhythm guitarists, such as Herb Ellis, try to create an actual melodic line in the top voice of the chords. Listen to any recording by Ellis and try to hear the little melodies he creates as he comps.

Below are several examples of this type of playing. All the chord forms used are shown on pages 86, 87, 88, and 89.

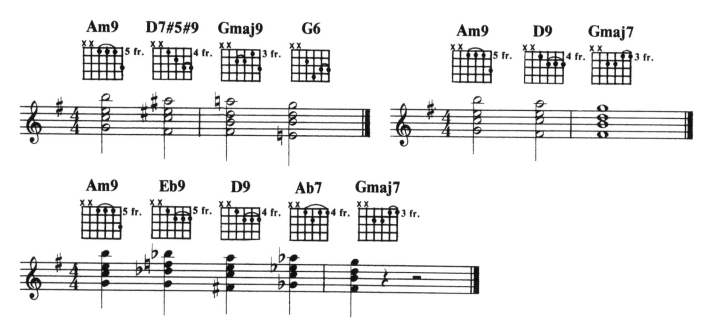

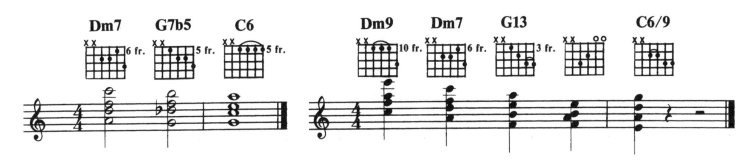

Note the use of the open strings in the G13. In recent years this kind of chord has gained great favor among many jazz guitarists.

The following is an example of a I–VI–II–V progression with a melody formed by the top voice in each chord. All the chord forms do not necessarily have a root. The root would be supplied by a bass player.

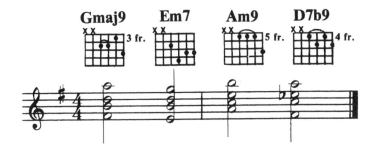

Here is another I–VI–II–V progression that requires a little more movement:

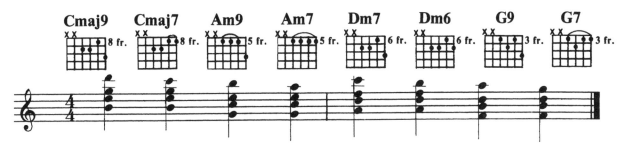

A variation on the above might be as follows:

The important thing to remember is that you wish to create an interesting melodic counter-line to what the soloist is doing *and* also keep the rhythmic background interesting.

Rhythmic Comping

The rhythmic variations that are possible while comping are almost unlimited. Most comping patterns are not pre-planned but are spontaneous responses to what the soloist is doing. However, you *can* practice some types of rhythm comps just to get the feel of what can be done. It is best to keep the voicings simple for now, so that you are not held back by your own limitations.

Sustained comps: This type of comping provides a nice cushion for the soloist to play on. It is usually played when the soloist is busy with a lot of notes. The more the soloist plays the less the accompanist should play. Do not be afraid to include some short syncopated chords along with the sustained chords to give a rhythmic lift or push.

Rhythmic pattern: **Applied to progression:**

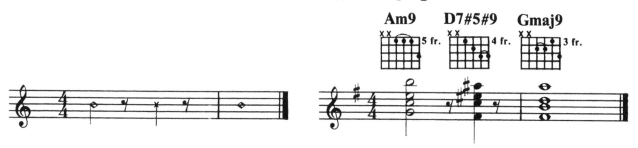

Rhythmic pattern:

Applied to progression:

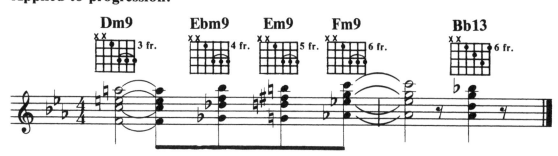

Rhythmic pattern:

Applied to progression:

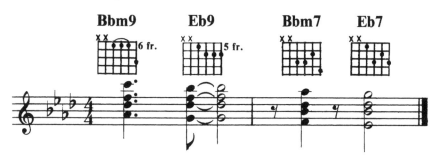

Rhythmic comps: These next comp patterns are more rhythmic than the sustained comps. Note the greater use of space between chords. It isn't necessary to play on every beat.

Rhythmic pattern:

Applied to progression:

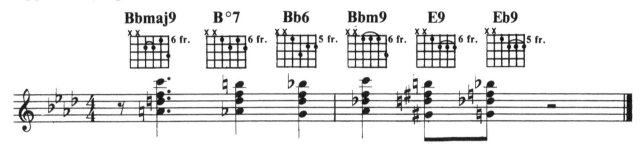

Notice that the B°7 is used to connect the two Bb chords creating a melody in the top voice. The E9 is also used as a half step approach chord to the Eb9 and again creates a melody in the top voice.

In the next example note the use of the common tone between the four chords.

Rhythmic pattern:

Applied to progression:

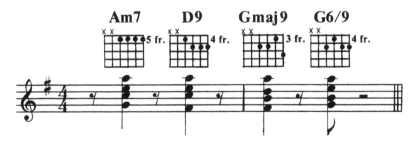

Blues Comps

Below is an example of what might be done when comping on a blues progression. Note the use of the common tone in the top voice through the first nine measures. In the tenth measure the descending diminished seventh chords act as a substitute for the D7 normally used in that measure.

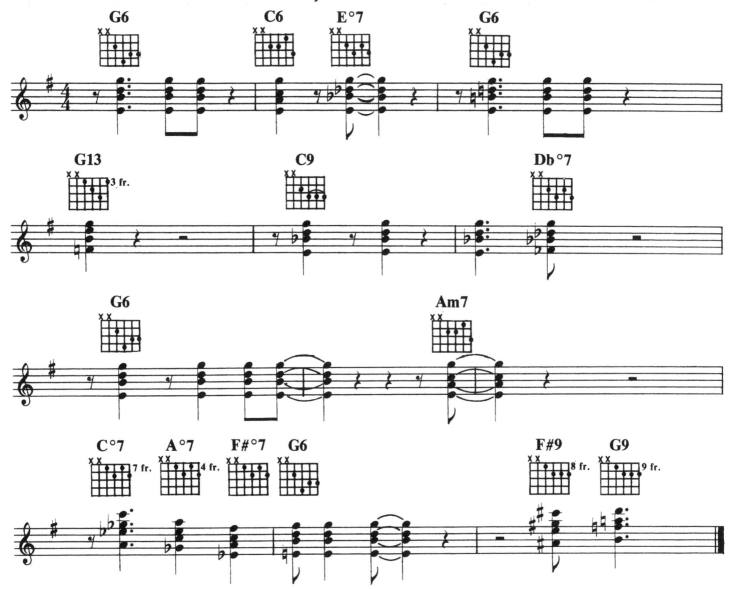

The following illustrates comping on a rather modern version of the blues progression. This progression was much favored by the musicians of the bop era of the 1940s. Notice that the rhythms are in sequential two measure patterns.

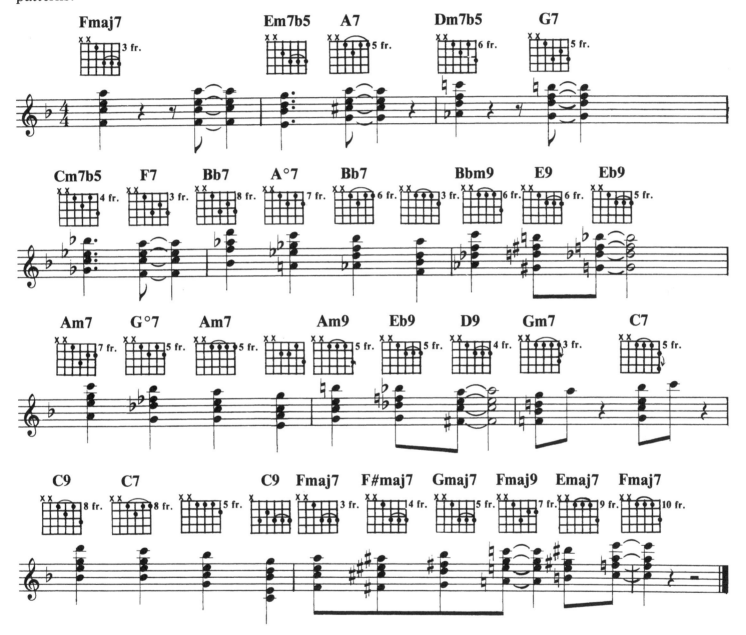

Blues with Two Chord Forms

These two chord forms are very useful because you can play through a complete blues progression using only these forms.

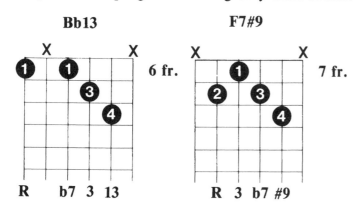

Obviously both forms are movable and you should be able to move them up and down the fingerboard and know the name of each chord at each fret.

Below is a blues progression in the key of F. Notice that the quality of all the chords is that of a dominant chord. This gives the progression a funkier feeling. Notice the use of the half step approach chords.

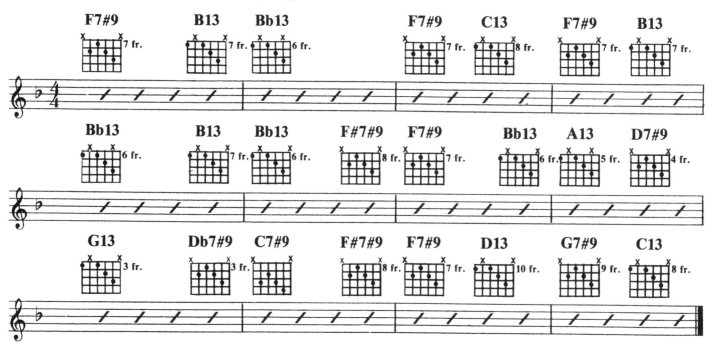

Using the same two chord forms, here is a blues in Bb. Note the extensive use of rhythms to create a more interesting background.

Blues with One Chord Form

Playing the blues can be further simplified by reducing the chord forms to just one, which is shown below. The root is now on the top string. You've played this chord form before.

G13

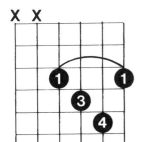

This one chord formation can be used to play through the entire blues progression.

Below is the same blues progression played on page 98 but using the thirteenth chord form shown here. *All* the roots are played on the first string.

We can take another step and reduce the chord form to three notes. If you look carefully at the fingering for the thirteenth chord form and the seventh sharped ninth chord form you will see that three of the notes are exactly the same.

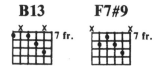

By omitting the root from both chord forms, what we have left can be either a thirteenth or a seventh sharped ninth. The form that we have can now be used throughout the entire blues progression. The diagrams below illustrate the three basic chords in the blues in Bb. Remember that the root of each chord must be visualized in your head.

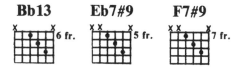

Two Note Chords

Let's take our study of comping chords one step further and reduce our three note chords to two notes. Although two notes are not usually referred to as a chord, for our purposes we will call them two note chords. The most important notes in any chord are the third and the seventh. These are often called the "color tones." They give the chord its quality, whether the chord is a major seventh, minor seventh, or dominant seventh. If we reduce our chords to just those two notes it can make our comping simpler and yet still provide the harmonic underpinning needed by the improvising musician.

Let's look once again at some of our basic chords. Note that the third and seventh of each chord are circled.

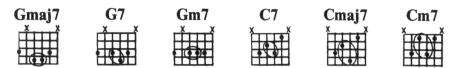

Now let's isolate the third and seventh of each of the above chords.

All of the above two note chords are movable and should be practiced all over the fingerboard. Go back over all the chord forms you have learned, isolate the thirds and sevenths and move them around the fingerboard.

Blues with Two Note Comps

Here is an example of two note comping on a Bb blues progression. Obviously
this works even better if a bass player is playing the roots of each chord.

Harmonic Movement and The Cycle

A very useful device for generating harmonic movement in a progression that is rather static is "the cycle." The cycle is based on the fact that there is a strong tendency for the root of a chord to progress down a perfect fifth or up a perfect fourth (depending in which direction you count). This is best demonstrated by the movement of the V chord to the I chord.

A logical extension of this relationship of V to I is when we place the II in front of the V (II–V–I). In the Dm7–G7–Cmaj7 progression, the roots of each chord move in a cyclical fashion. D to G is a fourth (or a fifth) and G to C is a fourth (or a fifth). To carry this principle a step further and to continue the cycle we can put a VI in front of the II. For example: Am7–Dm7–G7–Cmaj7. This progression is found in many, many standard tunes. It is usually written with the I chord as a starting point: Cmaj7–Am7–Dm7–G7, then starts again with Cmaj7. We can extend the cycle even further by substituting the III for the I chord as a starting point, giving us the progression III–VI–II–V–I. For example: Em7–Am7–Dm7–G7 and ending on Cmaj7. What is important at this point is that the principle of harmonic movement of chord roots a fourth upward (or a fifth downward), be thoroughly understood.

Application of The Cycle

Having accepted the fact that chords move in progressions based on intervals of perfect fourths upward (or perfect fifths downward), let's write out the complete series of roots through the cycle:

C–F–Bb–Eb–Ab– {Db} – {Gb} –B–E–A–D–G–C.
　　　　　　　　{C#}　　{F#}

Each of the above letters represents the root of a chord of some quality; major, minor, dominant, etc. In using the cycle to add chords to a progression, here is what we do. Suppose you have a progression such as the following:

It's obvious that the progression as it is is rather static. There is very little harmonic interest or movement. The progression begins on a Cmaj7 and moves to a G7 chord. G7 becomes our "goal" chord. The question is, what chord can we place in front of the G7? If we look at the cycle, we see that D is the chord that comes before G, so we can put a D chord in the measure before the G7. We now look for a chord that will bring us to the D chord and looking back at the cycle again we find that an A chord comes before the D so we can place an A chord in the second measure.

Here is the result:

Our fill-in chords are both major but now we can change the quality of the chords to what sounds best. Below are some possibilities:

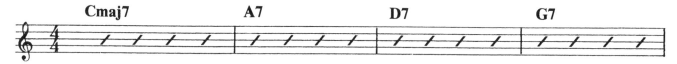

In the above progression, the series of dominant seventh chords gives a greater sense of harmonic motion. The A7 to the D7 to the G7 is thought of as V of V of V. Each chord is the V of the next chord.

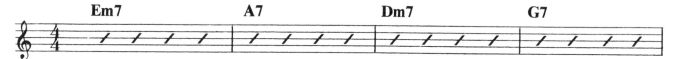

By using the Am7 and the Dm7 we have a I–VI–II–V progression which keeps the progression in the key of C while still retaining the harmonic motion. In the previous progression, by making the chords into dominants we actually have different key feelings in each measure.

In the progression above by using the III chord as a substitute for the I (Em7 for the Cmaj7) and changing the Am7 to A7, we now have a II–V progression, followed by Dm7–G7, which is another II–V progression. Of the three possibilities the determining factor is the sound. You have to be the final judge. If there is no conflict with whatever melody is being played over the progression, then you can use whichever you want. Let your ears tell you.

Backcycling

The process just described to fill in chords in a progression which had very little harmonic movement is called ''backcycling.'' Below are the first five measures of a simple blues progression. There is no harmonic movement between the Cmaj7 and the F chord. The assignment is to create more motion from the Cmaj7 to the ''goal'' chord, the F.

Think of the F chord as a temporary I chord and the cycle tells you that a C7 chord will lead to the F, also that a Gm7 (II–V) can be placed before the C7.

Cmaj7   **Gm7**   **C7**   **F**

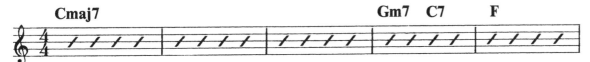

Think of the Gm7 as the new "goal" chord or as a temporary I, and looking back at the cycle you will see that a D7 will lead to the Gm7. In front of the D7 you can place an Am7 (II–V). The Am7 is also part of the cycle (A–D–G–C–F).

Cmaj7   **Am7**   **D7**   **Gm7**   **C7**   **F**

Now you can go another step and think of the Am7 as a temporary I chord or a "goal" chord. Looking back at the cycle you will see an E7 leads to the Am7. Again we can place the Bm7 (II–V) in front of the E7. The progression is complete. Notice how much more movement you have in going from the original Cmaj7 to the F chord.

Cmaj7   **Bm7**   **E7**   **Am7**   **D7**   **Gm7**   **C7**   **F**

The principles of chord embellishment can be applied to the new chord progression, so that you may have something that looks like this.

Cmaj9   **Bm7b5** **E7b9**   **Am7**   **D7b9**   **Gm7b5** **C7#9** **C7b9** **Fmaj7**

Chord Melody Solos

Playing chord melody solos is probably the most challenging and the most satisfying of all the different ways in which the guitar can be played. If you're not exactly sure of what chord melody playing is let me explain. Chord melody is the term used to describe the combining of chords and melody. The guitarist is the soloist and the accompanist at the same time. In the last section we discussed comping and creating a melody in the top voice of the chords. In chord melody playing we are given a melody and have to add chords to it. The melody is again the top note and we have to play our chords in such a way that the given melody notes are in the top voice of each chord.

Basic Principles of Chord Melody Playing

Any melody that we are going to play must, for the most part, be played on the first and second strings. The purpose of this is to have enough strings below the melody so that we can get a full sounding chord. Therefore, if the melody is written too low we must raise it an octave higher.

The notes which make up the melody are usually one of the notes of the basic chord or a note is an extended or altered note of the basic chord. You must be able to relate the melody note to its numbered position within the chord. For example, if the melody note is D on the fourth line of the staff, and the chord is a G7, you must automatically know that D is the fifth of the G7 chord and be able to play a G7 with the fifth on top. The diagram below illustrates the chord form.

 This note is played using this form:

Suppose that the melody note is an E on the fourth space of the staff and the chord symbol is G7. You have to know that the E would be the thirteenth of the G7 chord and to play the G13 chord which places the E on the second string.

 This note is played using this form. It is the G7 extended to a G13, sometimes called a G7/6:

Before trying your first chord melody solo let's have a few more examples. Suppose the melody note is G above the staff, and the chord symbol is just the letter G. The letter G without anything next to it such as 7 or 9 etc. indicates a pure G chord. Since the G is the root of the G chord we must know a chord form that places the root on the top of the chord.

 This note could be played using any of the following chord forms: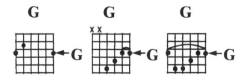

If you want to make the melody a little more modern sounding you can play a Gmaj7, a G6 or a G6/9:

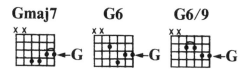

If the melody note is G and the chord symbol is C#7, the G would be the flatted fifth of the C#m7 chord so you must know a form for the C#m7b5 that places the G on the top. The C#m7b5 is of course an altered chord which is necessary to harmonize the note G.

This note is played using either of the following chord forms:

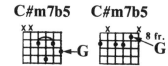

If the melody note is G and the chord symbol is Ebmaj7, the G is the third of the Ebmaj7 and you must know a form of the chord which places the third on the top.

This note can be played using any of the following chord forms:

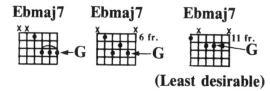

(Least desirable)

When given a choice of which chord form to use, it is best to use the form which is closest to the nut since it allows more of the string to vibrate creating a livelier sound.

Aura Lee

For our first example of a chord melody solo I've chosen a traditional melody which goes back to the days of the Civil War. It's called "Aura Lee."

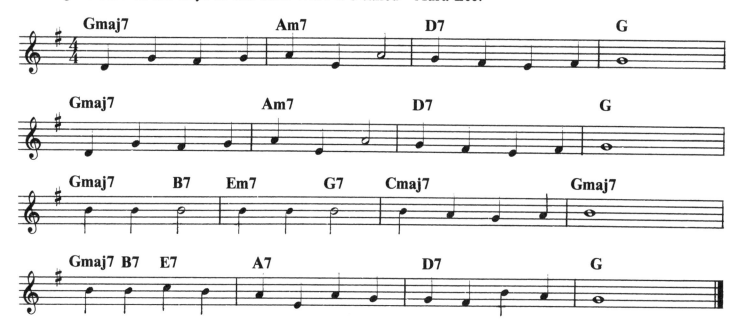

The first thing you must do is to raise the melody an octave higher so that there is room under the melody to place the chords. It isn't necessary to harmonize or play a chord for every note, usually when playing a song which contains four beats to each measure you can put a chord on the first and third beats in each measure. Of course this is subject to your own personal taste. Where there is only one note to a measure, such as in measures four and eight, you can break up the chord by adding other chords or improvising a melodic fill in. The following is a chord melody solo on the tune "Aura Lee." The chord diagrams will help you to better understand the relationship between the melody notes and the chord forms. An analysis will follow.

Aura Lee

(Chord Melody Solo)

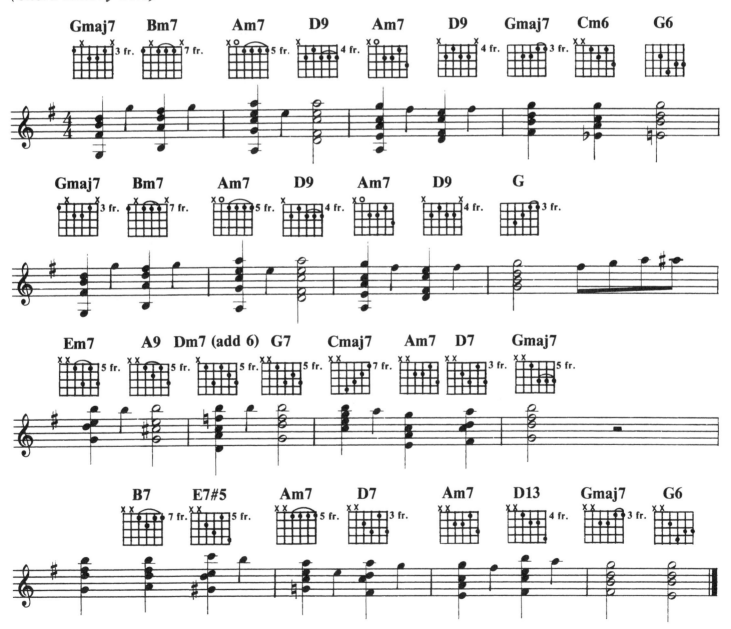

Analysis of "Aura Lee" Chord Melody Solo

One of the most important factors in creating a chord melody solo is to have good sounding chord changes to harmonize the melody that you're working on. The following analysis will help to explain the chords used in the chord solo just played.

Measures 1, 5, 12, 13, and 16: The Gmaj7 chords are used in place of the original G chords to produce a more modern sound.

Measures 1 and 5: The Bm7 is a III chord in the key of G and is a substitute for the G chord. It harmonizes the melody F# very well. A Gmaj7 with the seventh (F#) on the top could also have been used.

Measures 2, 3, 6, 7, 14, and 15: When there is a II-V progression for two measures using the II-V in each measure adds greater color. Also the Am7 in the third measure harmonizes the note G very well, and the D9 harmonizes the note E very well. In the fifteenth measure the note B is the thirteenth of the D7 chord.

Measure 4: The Cm6 is used to break up the sound of the I chord. It is a I-IVm6-I progression. This works best when the melody note is sustained.

Measure 8: The melodic fill in is used as a lead into the next measure.

Measures 9 and 10: The Em7 is the VI chord substitution for the original G chord (VI substitutes for I). The A9 is used to prepare for the Dm7 in the next measure. Also, the melody note B is the ninth of the A7 chord. The Dm7 chord is used to prepare for the G7. The add 6 is used to accommodate the melody note B.

Measure 11: The Am7-D7 is a II-V progression which prepares for the Gmaj7 in the following measure.

Measure 13: The E7#5 is used to accommodate the melody note C. The C is the raised or sharped fifth of the chord. This is another example of altering a chord to harmonize a note which is not in the basic chord.

Measure 16: The G6 is used because a major sixth is often used to resolve a major seventh.

I'm sure that at this point you've come to realize how important it is to review all the chord forms you've learned and to know which note is the top voice. This is important whether you are comping or playing chord melody solos. I must stress that to harmonize any given melody note you must know what the relative position of the melody note is to the given chord symbol and be able to play the chord form that has that melody note in the top voice.

To illustrate further the art of creating chord melody playing here is one more example, the traditional folk song "Greensleeves."

Greensleeves

Below is a chord melody solo based on "Greensleeves." The melody is raised an octave and there is extensive use of substitute chords and cyclical movement. An analysis with full explanations will follow.

Greensleeves

(Chord Melody Solo)

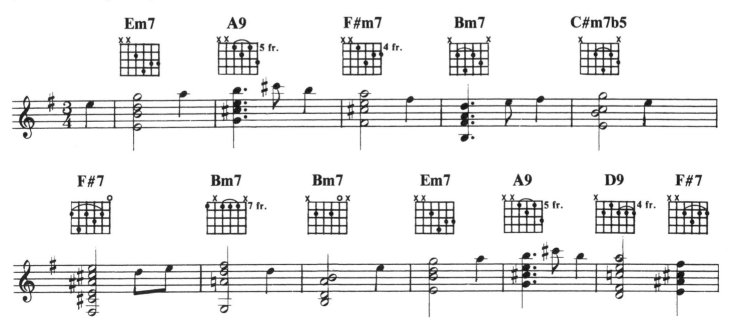

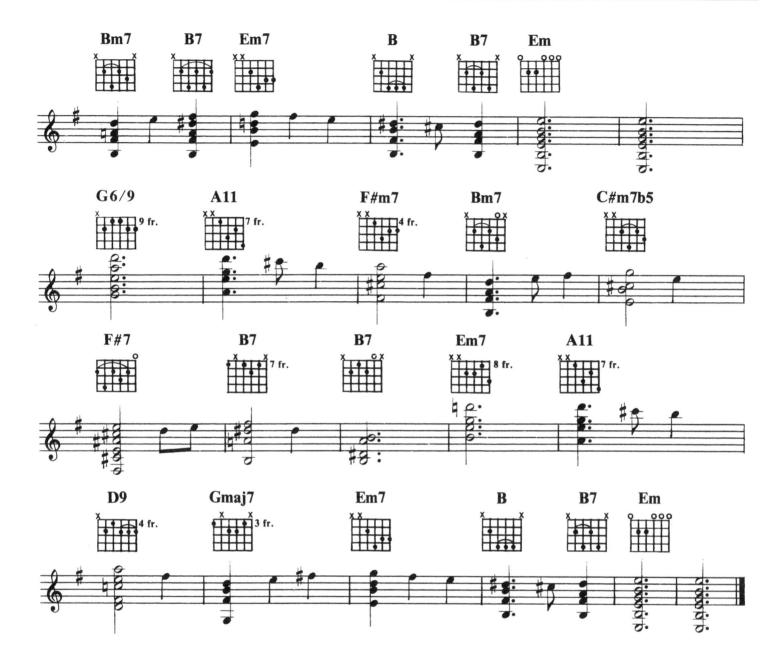

Analysis of "Greensleeves" Chord Melody Solo

The following analysis will help you to better understand the reasoning for the substitutions and fill in chords. Compare the progression shown below with the original progression on page 109.

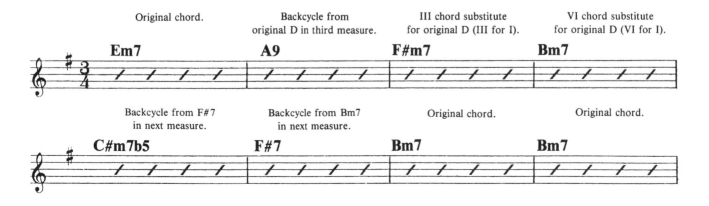

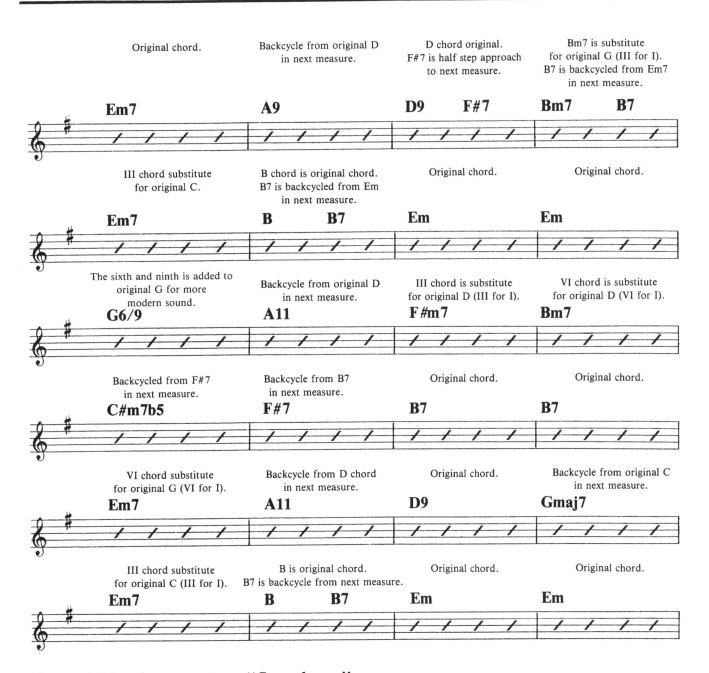

Some additional comments on "Greensleeves":

In the second measure the A9 is used because of backcycling from the original D in the third measure. This is possible even though the D is replaced with its own substitute F#m7. The ninth is used in order to accommodate the melody note B which is the ninth of the A chord. Another way of thinking of the A9 is as the V of the original D chord. That is the same reasoning for the A9 in the tenth measure. The F#7 in the eleventh measure is the half step approach to the G chord which was in the original progression. However, in the twelfth measure the Bm7 is used as a substitute for the original G chord (III for I) and you can think of the F#7 as backcycling from the Bm7, or as the V of the Bm7. Remember that you can think of almost any chord as a *temporary I* and put a V chord in front of it. Continuing with that same line of thinking, the B7 in the twelfth measure is a result of backcycling from the Em7 in the following measure. It may also be thought of as the V chord to the Em7 (temporary I) chord. After a while this kind of thinking will come easier to you.

Basic Triads and Chord Melody Solos

Earlier we learned that a triad is a three note chord containing a root, third and fifth. Because of the very pure sound of the triad it is best used when harmonizing simple tunes whose very beauty lies in their simplicity.

Let's learn some of the more widely used triads. Play each of the following chord forms up the fingerboard and name each chord as you go up.

Major Triads

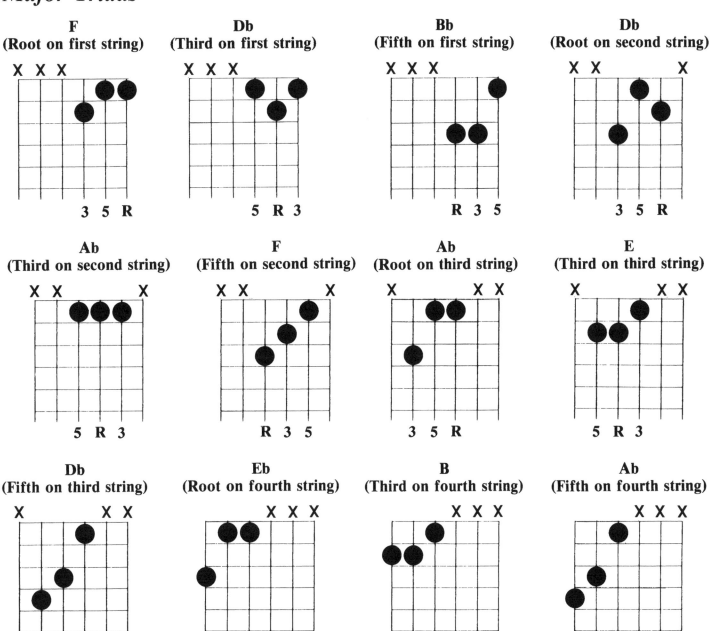

F
(Root on first string)
3 5 R

Db
(Third on first string)
5 R 3

Bb
(Fifth on first string)
R 3 5

Db
(Root on second string)
3 5 R

Ab
(Third on second string)
5 R 3

F
(Fifth on second string)
R 3 5

Ab
(Root on third string)
3 5 R

E
(Third on third string)
5 R 3

Db
(Fifth on third string)
R 3 5

Eb
(Root on fourth string)
3 5 R

B
(Third on fourth string)
5 R 3

Ab
(Fifth on fourth string)
R 3 5

Minor Triads

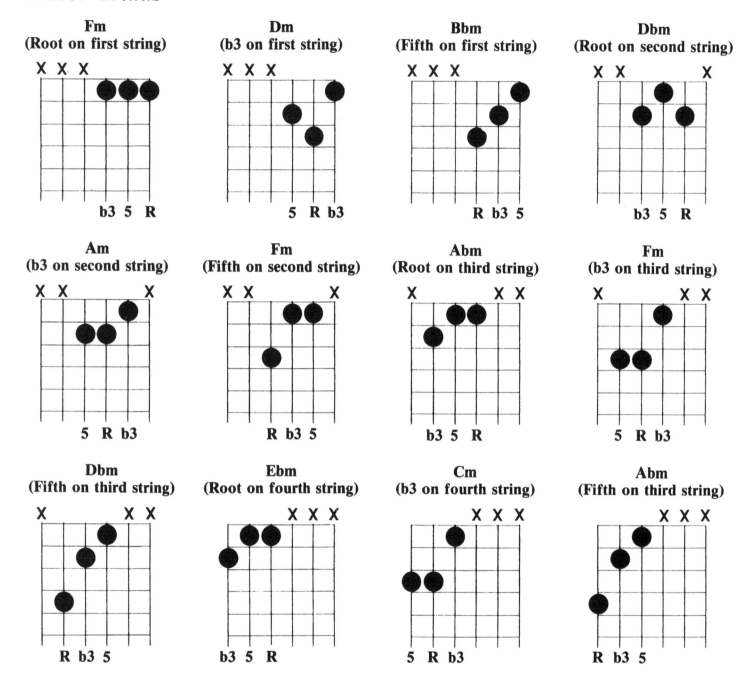

Augmented Triads

Augmented triads are formed by *raising* the fifth of each chord form.

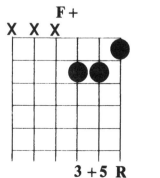
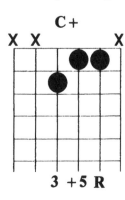

Because of the construction of the augmented chord each of the notes in the chord may be considered the root. The F+ triad may also be thought of as the A+ or the C#+.

Diminished Triads

Diminished triads are formed by *lowering* the third and fifth of each chord form.

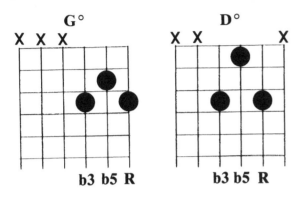

The diminished triads also have three possible names. Each of the notes in the triad may be considered the root. For example, the G° may also be thought of as the Bb° or the Db°.

The following traditional folk song is used to illustrate the use of triadic harmony. Included among the triads are a number of full four note chords, which provides an interesting contrast to the three note chords.

Home on the Range

(Chord Melody Solo)

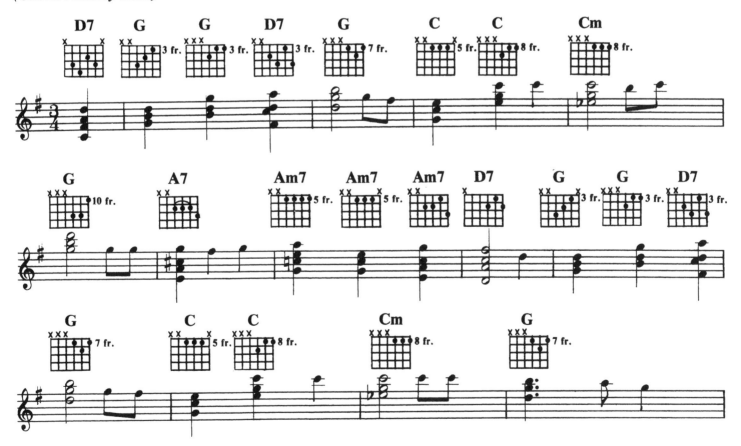

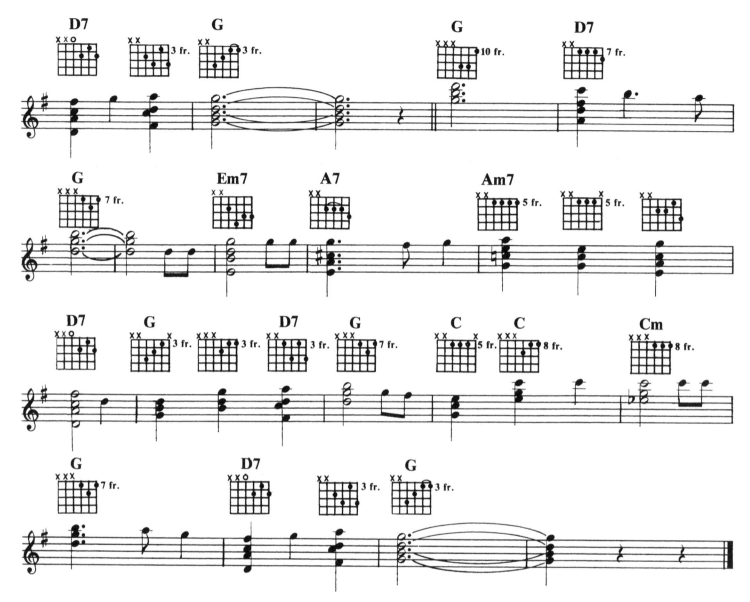

For further practice, take other folk songs and play chord melody solos based on those songs.

Resolution of Augmented Triads

The augmented triad is composed of all major thirds therefore any note of the triad may be considered the root. For example a C + triad may also be considered an E + or an Ab + . The augmented triad is often used as a substitute for a dominant seventh chord and has a strong pull to the tonic (I) triad. Below are three examples:

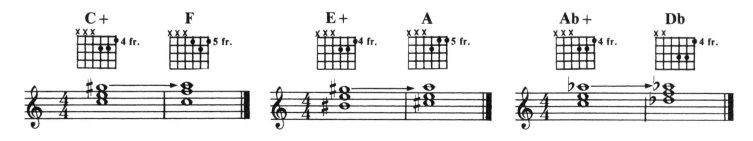

Minor Chords with a Descending Chromatic Line

A very popular minor chord sequence is the minor–minor (major seven)–minor seven–minor six progression. This progression is heard in such tunes as "Michelle," "More," "My Funny Valentine," "What Are You Doing the Rest of Your Life?" and many other popular standard tunes. The beauty of this chord sequence is in the descending chromatic line which is indicated in the chord symbols. Below are several examples of how this progression is fingered.

In this first example listen to the descending chromatic line on the third string:

Cm   Cm (maj7)   Cm7   Cm6

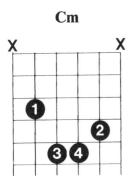 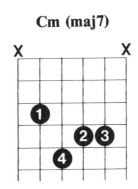 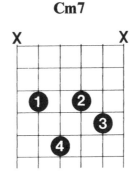 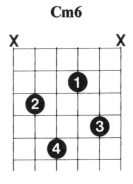

Now the descending chromatic line is on the fourth string.

Gm   Gm (maj7)   Gm7   Gm6

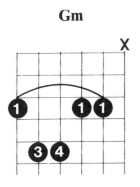 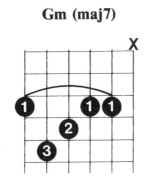 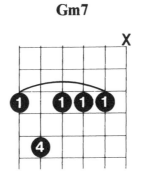 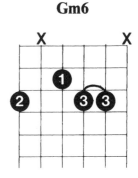

In the next example, the descending chromatic line is again on the fourth string, but easier to hear because it is in an outside voice and not buried in the middle of the chord.

Gm   Gm (maj7)   Gm7   Gm6

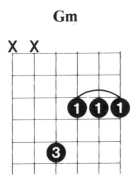 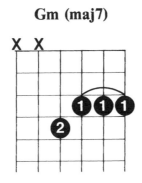 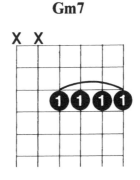 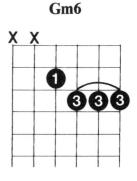

This last example has the descending chromatic line on the sixth string.

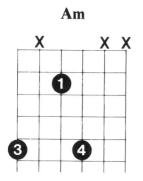
Am

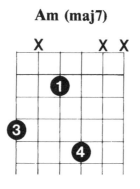
Am (maj7)

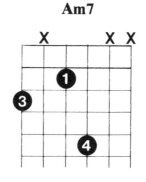
Am7

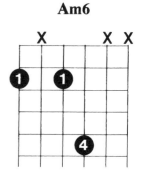
Am6

Occasionally the second chord in the minor chord sequence, the minor (major 7), is shown as an augmented chord:

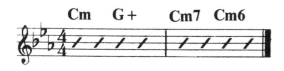
Cm   G+   Cm7   Cm6

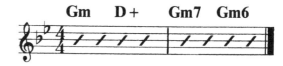
Gm   D+   Gm7   Gm6

Although the augmented chord is given you should play the progression as shown below:

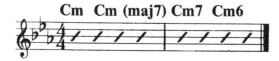
Cm Cm (maj7) Cm7 Cm6

Gm Gm (maj7) Gm7 Gm6

The minor chord sequence that you've just learned may also be used in the normal II–V progression as shown below.

Given progression:

Am7   D7   Gmaj7 G6

May be played as this:

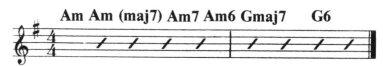
Am Am (maj7) Am7 Am6 Gmaj7   G6

The Am6 is a D9 which takes the place of the D7 chord. The same progression may be played in four measures like this:

Am7   D7   Gmaj7   G6

Using the minor chord sequence we have the following:

Am   Am (maj7) Am7   Am6   Gmaj7   G6

Triads and Slash Chords

In the late 1960s a new way of writing chord symbols became very popular and it is important for any guitarist involved in contemporary music, pop, rock, fusion, etc. to understand what these new chord symbols mean.

Below are several examples of what these new chord symbols look like:

C/G   Bb/A   F/C   F/A   D/F#   C/A

The chords, sometimes referred to as slash chords, indicate that a triad is played over a particular bass note. For example, C/G tells you that a C triad is played with the note G in the bass. While this may appear to be simple, it can, in fact, be rather tricky, especially if you come across them in a situation where you have no time to work out the fingerings.

Below are a number of examples of slash chords. In the chord diagrams, the bass note is indicated with an open circle.

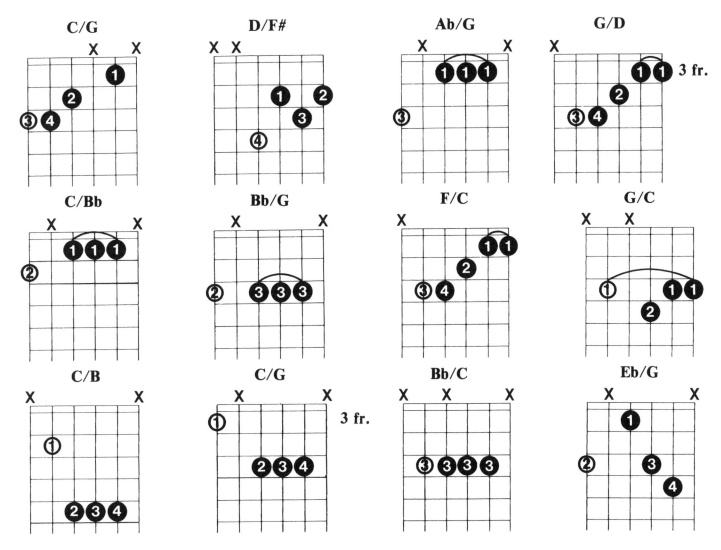

You must certainly recognize many of the above chord forms as forms you've already learned, however, you should be acquainted with the new way of writing them. At this point you should practice making up your own chord forms. Take any major or minor triad and try playing that triad over every note in the chromatic scale. You will come across forms that you have never had before and it will help you to learn the fingerboard even better.

Open String Jazz Chords

Another group of chords which are increasingly being used are the open string jazz chords. These chord forms allow you to play voicings with intervallic spacings that are not normally playable.

Below is a form for an Amaj9 chord:

Here is another fingering for the Amaj9 which makes use of open strings:

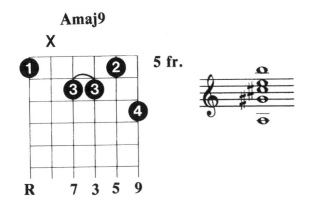

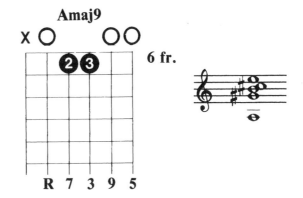

Note the obvious ease in fingering the open string Amaj9 and also the unusual sound of this new voicing which contains the interval of a major second between the B and the C#.

Here are two more open string chords which are variations of the form above:

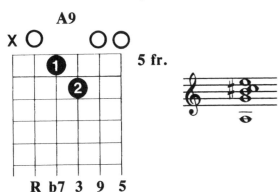

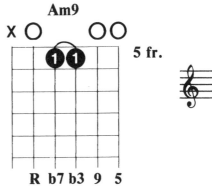

The important thing to remember is that the first and second strings, the E and B strings, must be made to fit into chords that you already know. They may be some extended or altered notes of chords that you've already learned. Here is a brief listing of some possible open string chords:

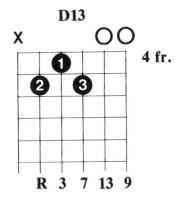

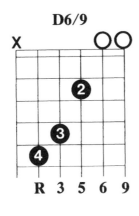

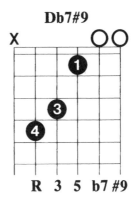

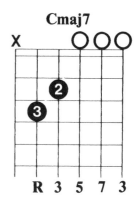

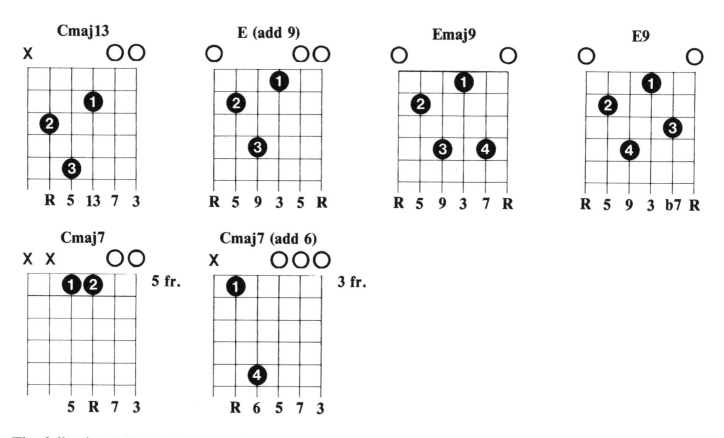

The following I–VI–II–V progressions are made up of open string chord forms.

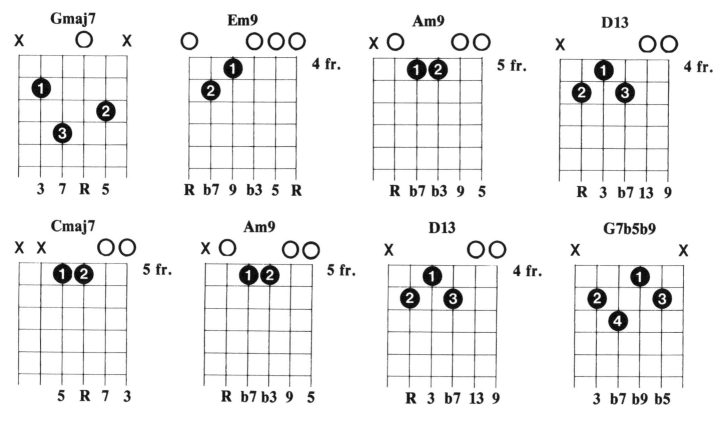

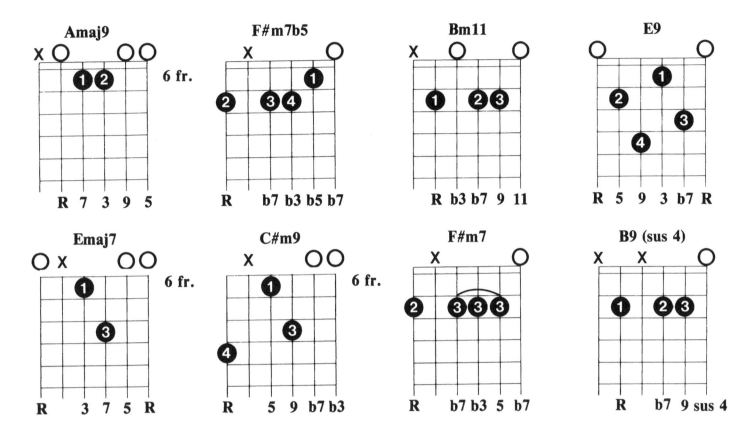

The above are just a small sampling of what can be done with open string chords. By careful concentration and experimenting, you should be able to discover many more unusual chord formations and add much interest to your playing. Remember that the sixth, fifth, and fourth strings are generally roots and the first, second, and even the third strings may be the altered strings of some chord.

Appendix

The following additional information might be helpful in reaching an even greater understanding of the material just covered.

Half Step:

A half step is the smallest distance between two notes. On the guitar fingerboard a half step would be one fret up or down. For example: C–C#; E–F; B–C.

Whole Step:

A whole step is equal to two half steps. On the guitar fingerboard a whole step would be two frets up or down. For example: C–D, E–F#, B–C#.

Intervals:

An interval is the distance from one note to another note. The distance is measured by counting up from the lower note to the higher note. From C to E is an interval of a third, from A to E is a fifth, from F to E is a seventh.

Intervals in the Major Scale:

The following illustrates the intervals from the tonic of the major scale to any other note within the scale. Although the illustration is shown in the key of C major, the same intervals apply to all major scales.

Unison	Second	Third	Fourth	Fifth	Sixth	Seventh	Octave

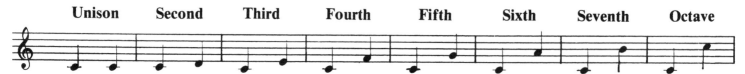

Although intervals are usually counted upward as shown above, they may also be counted downward. Going down from G to C is an interval of a fifth (G–F–E–D–C).

In counting the letters in order to determine the interval, sharps and flats are not figured in the interval distance. For example:

C to E is a third
C to Eb is a third
C# to E is a third

Interval Type:

It should be obvious from the examples shown above that there must be some difference in the kinds of thirds that are possible. If we count up from C to E in terms of whole steps and half steps we find that C to E is made up of two whole steps. This is a major third. Counting from C to Eb we find that it is made up of a whole step and a half step. This is a minor third. C# to E is also made up of a whole step and a half step and is a minor third. From this we can conclude that besides the interval number (second, third, fourth, etc.) all intervals belong to a particular quality or type. Below we see the C major scale with its different interval qualities.

Unison Major Second Major Third Perfect Fourth Perfect Fifth Major Sixth Major Seventh Octave

In all major scales all seconds, thirds, sixths and sevenths are major intervals. Fourths, fifths and octaves are perfect intervals.

All interval types may be changed by lowering or raising one of the notes of the interval. The following rules determine how to alter an interval:

When a major interval is made smaller (lowered) by a half step it becomes minor.

When a major interval is made larger (raised) by a half step it becomes augmented.

When a perfect interval is made larger by a half step it becomes augmented.

When a perfect interval is made smaller by a half step it becomes diminished.

When a minor interval becomes smaller by a half step it becomes diminished.

Chord Interval Structures

Most chords are based on intervals of thirds, though some jazz artists have experimented with chords based on intervals of a fourth. Below we see the intervallic structure of some of the basic chord structures.

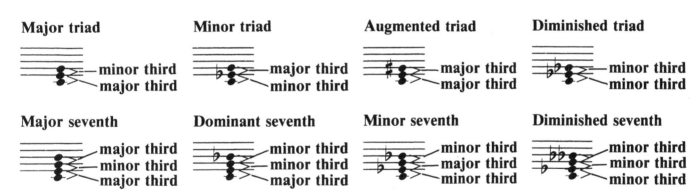